£2
20

*Still
in Bed
with an
Elephant*

Other books by Paul Henderson Scott

1707: The Union of Scotland and England (1979)
Walter Scott and Scotland (1981)
John Galt (1985)
In Bed with an Elephant (1985)
The Thinking Nation (1989)
Cultural Independence (1989)
Towards Independence: Essays on Scotland (1991)
Andrew Fletcher and the Treaty of Union (1992)
Scotland in Europe: A Dialogue with a Sceptical Friend (1992)
Defoe in Edinburgh and Other Papers (1995)
A Mad God's Dream (1997)

Edited

(with A.C. Davies) The Age of MacDiarmid (1980)
Sir Walter Scott's *The Letters of Malachi Malagrowther* (1981)
Andrew Fletcher's *United and Separate Parliaments* (1982)
(with George Bruce) A Scottish Postbag (1986)
(with A.C. Davies) Policy for the Arts: a selection
of AdCAS Papers (1991)
Scotland: A Concise Cultural History (1993)
(with Daniel Szechi) *Scotland's Ruine*: Lockhart of Carnwath's
Memoirs of the Union (1995)
(with Ian Gordon) John Galt's *The Member* and *The Radical* (1996)
Scotland: An Unwon Cause (1997)

Still in Bed
with an
Elephant

Paul Henderson Scott

THE SALTIRE SOCIETY

In Bed with an Elephant first published 1985 by The Saltire Society
Still in Bed with an Elephant: this revised edition with
additional material published 1998 by
The Saltire Society
9 Fountain Close,
22 High Street, Edinburgh EH1 1TF

A catalogue record for this book is available
from the British Library.

ISBN 0 85411 073 9

Cover Design by James Hutcheson

Printed and bound in Scotland by Bell & Bain Limited

Contents

Introduction

In Bed with an Elephant was first published by the Saltire Society in 1985 and it was reprinted by Polygon in *Towards Independence* in 1991. It is still in demand and the Society has therefore decided to issue a new edition. They have asked me to add some subsequent essays on the same theme, the effect on Scotland of sharing an island with a larger neighbour.

In 1995 Ludovic Kennedy used the same title for a book of his own, although he acknowledged in it that I had already used the title for what he called my "admirable Saltire Society booklet". Partly to avoid confusion, and to make the point that we are not yet out of the bed, we call the present collection, *Still in Bed with an Elephant*. The restoration of the Scottish Parliament is a decisive step forward, but with so many powers reserved to Westminster, we are still far from the satisfaction and security of our own room in the European mansion.

P.H.S.
Edinburgh
June 1998

Acknowledgements

I am grateful to the editors of the publications in which some of these papers have appeared, as indicated in each case. *In Bed with an Elephant* was reprinted in *Towards Independence, Essays on Scotland* (Polygon, Edinburgh, 1991 and 1996). *"A Severed and withered branch": The Rise and Fall of Britishness* was included in the proceedings of the Fourth International Scottish Studies Symposium, Universität Mainz in Germersheim. *From Scotland to Slovenia*, edited by H. W. Drescher and S. Hagemann, (Peter Lang, Frankfurt am Main, 1996), and *Robert Burns, Patriot* in those of the International Bicentenary Burns Conference in Strathclyde University, 1996, *Love and Liberty*, edited by Kenneth Simpson, (Tuckwell Press, 1997).

P.H.S.

IN BED WITH AN ELEPHANT

The Three Hundred Years' War

It was Pierre Trudeau, I believe, who said that for Canada to share a continent with the United States was like a man having to share a bed with an elephant. It is an experience which can be dangerous or very uncomfortable and lead to pressures which are difficult to avoid or resist. The elephant can use its sheer bulk and weight to flatten resistance altogether. This can happen even by accident without any malicious intention. If there is a conflict of interests or of tastes, weight is liable to predominate. This sort of experience is common whenever a country has a neighbour much larger and wealthier than itself. The world is full of examples, but one which has a longer history than most, some 700 years at least, is the case of Scotland and England. I should like to look at this example, which affects almost every aspect of our lives. It is a long and continuing story and, to understand it at all, it is necessary to begin with a little history.

The relationship between Scotland and England is the oldest of its kind in Europe, because they were the first countries to consolidate within very much the same borders as still exist. You could trace this border back to the time of the Roman Empire because it closely coincides with Hadrian's Wall. At all events, by the end of the thirteenth century both Scotland and England were relatively consolidated and prosperous states, living in relative peace and harmony with one another. This was an era which came to an abrupt end with the accidental death of King Alexander III of Scotland in 1286. The oldest surviving Scottish poem looks back to his reign as a lost Golden Age, because Edward I of England seized the opportunity of the disputed succession to attempt to take over Scotland, first by diplomatic manipulation and then, when that failed, by force. It was a pattern that was to be repeated frequently for the next 300 years, with the slaughter and destruction renewed in each attack.

The destructive effects of this prolonged attempt to conquer or subvert Scotland are beyond calculation; it was the longest war in European history. English historians, to their credit, have written some of the strongest condemnations of it. Henry Thomas Buckle, for example:

> The darling object of the English, was to subjugate the Scotch; and if anything could increase the disgrace of so base an enterprise, it would have been that, having undertaken it, they ignominiously failed.[1]

Or James Anthony Froude:

> The English hated Scotland because Scotland had successfully defied them: the Scots hated England as an enemy on the watch to make them slaves. The hereditary hostility strengthened with time, and each generation added fresh injuries to the accumulation of bitterness.[2]

It was the misfortune of Scotland to have on her border a country which was not only larger, and therefore more powerful, but which was, for centuries, particularly aggressive and expansionist. Scotland, Wales, Ireland and France were all exposed to repeated English efforts to subjugate them, with varying degrees of success. Every country within reach was fair game. Scotland had the further misfortune that the richest part of the country in the south was the most exposed to English attack and was frequently laid waste.

The national consciousness of Scotland, tempered in the crucible of this long struggle, found early expression in three notable documents. The first of these, the Declaration of Arbroath of 1320, was a diplomatic despatch in Latin. It was outstanding among such documents for its eloquence and passion but also for the startling originality, at such an early date, of its political ideas. The orthodox view among modern historians is that the idea of national self-determination evolved at about the time of the French Revolution with Rousseau's doctrine that sovereignty resides in the people and not the ruler. About 400 years before Rousseau, the same fundamental philosophy is expressed clearly and powerfully in this Declaration. Scotland is the oldest nation in Europe because it was the first to evolve two related ideas: that the distinctiveness of a national community is worth defending for its own sake, and that rulers exist to serve the community and not the reverse. There is a paragraph in the Declaration where these two ideas are combined. The previous passage refers to the appointment of Robert as King "with the due consent and assent of us all". It then continues:

> Yet if he should give up what he has begun, and agree to make us or our kingdom subject to the King of England or the English, we should exert ourselves at once to drive him out as our enemy and a subverter of his own rights and ours, and make some other man who was well able to defend us our King; for, as long as but a hundred of us remain alive, never will we on any conditions be brought under English rule. It is in truth not for glory, nor riches, nor honours that we are fighting, but for freedom — for that alone, which no honest man gives up but with life itself.[3]

The constitutional principles of the Declaration of Arbroath have never ceased to strike echoes in Scotland. Let me give only one example. In his novel, *Ringan Gilhaize*, John Galt is concerned to justify the resort by the Covenanters to "the divine right of resistance" against established authority. He recalls the Declaration in support and, to make sure that the reader does not miss the point, prints the whole text as an appendix. Scottish constitutional theory has always tended to reject the notions that sovereignty resided with a King or with Parliament or with any institution other than the whole community. It follows from this that there is a manifest right to resist injustice from whatever source it comes. Another implication is the egalitarian view that all men have equal rights. This is another assumption which from these early times has strongly influenced Scottish attitudes to politics and religion.

The other two documents which emerged from the struggle for independence are works of a very different character from the Declaration, but they are imbued with the same spirit: the two long narrative or epic poems, Barbour's *Brus* and Hary's *Wallace*.

They are two of the earliest surviving works of Scottish literature. So it is a literature which virtually began with the celebration of the two national heroes of the War of Independence and with the assertion and elaboration of the ideas of the Declaration of Arbroath. The two poems have had a long-continuing influence, directly and indirectly. Until about the end of the eighteenth century, versions of them were among the most widely read books in Scotland. They in turn influenced other writers who continued to be read long after Barbour and Hary themselves had been relegated to the specialists. Robert Burns, for example, in his famous autobiographical letter to John Moore said: "The story of Wallace poured a Scottish prejudice in my veins which will boil along there till the flood-gates of life shut in eternal rest".[4] Many other people have said much the same. It is by such means as these that the epic Scottish struggle for independence has passed into legend or folk memory and helped to shape instinctive attitudes and responses.

One of the consequences of the long war of resistance against England was that Scotland was encouraged to seek markets, allies and cultural and intellectual exchange with continental Europe. For centuries, Scottish merchants, soldiers and scholars travelled everywhere, from Scandinavia to Italy, from Portugal to Russia. Many established themselves in country after country as generals, ambassadors, architects or professors. The contribution which many of these men made to the development of other countries in Europe is very remarkable. Take, for example, James Keith, exiled from Scotland for his Jacobitism. In Russia, he became a general at the age of 32, then ambassador to Sweden and governor of the Ukraine. He left the Russian service to became the right-hand man and field-marshal of Frederick the Great. His brother, George, Earl Marischal of Scotland, was the Prussian Ambassador to Spain, Governor of Neuchatel and the only man to win the unqualified approval of Rousseau. Patrick Gordon, another native of Buchan, also became a Russian General and he was a key figure in the transformation of Russia under Peter the Great. "After the Czar himself," John Hill Burton wrote, "it may be questioned if any other man did so much for the early consolidation of the Russian empire."[5] John Law of Lauriston shaped French financial policy and founded the Bank of France. George Buchanan, who wrote in Latin (one of the four languages of Scottish literature) was regarded as the leading poet in Europe, "poetarum nostri saeculi facile princeps." He was not only Principal of St. Leonard's College in St. Andrews, but at various times an intellectual force in the universities of Paris, Bordeaux and Coimbra in Portugal. These are only a few random examples from different countries and periods of the intimate Scottish relationship with Europe. Above all we had a close alliance with France for over 300 years, so close that the two countries exchanged citizenship and Scots formed the guard of the French Kings. We were actively and consciously European centuries before the EEC.

This Scottish involvement with the rest of Europe was so different from the much more insular and self-sufficient attitude of England that it alone accounts for many of the radical differences between the Scottish and English traditions. The Scottish interchange with other countries in Europe brought foreign influence at its most stimulating and beneficial. It was diverse and accepted on its merits, not monolithic and imposed; it was quite different from suffocation by elephantine weight. Every aspect of life in Scotland from music and dance to architecture and law was affected by this European influence. In particular, the universities from the fifteenth century onwards developed in close touch with intellectual movements in the rest of Europe. Scottish scholars went, as a matter of course, to study and teach in the universities of France, Italy, Germany and the Low Countries. Many of them brought back new ideas to Scotland. Dugald Stewart, the first historian of the Scottish Enlightenment, had no doubt that its origins were to be found, at least partly, in this "constant influx of information and of liberality from abroad"[6] during the previous centuries. The Enlightenment was the culmination of a long process, not a sudden and mysterious apparition.

In spite of the constant devastation and wastage of the long war with England, the achievements of the medieval Scottish kingdom were considerable. They reached their highest point towards the end of the fifteenth century during the reign of James IV, a true Renaissance prince. It was the age of Henryson, Dunbar and Douglas, whose poetry was among the most impressive written in Europe in that century. Their language was Middle Scots, a rich and expressive tongue, used for all purposes and at all social levels. It was an age also of intellectual and artistic innovation in many diverse directions and of active involvement in European diplomacy. The demands of the French alliance led to the campaign which ended disastrously at the Battle of Flodden in 1513. So ended, abruptly, the bright hopes of the fifteenth-century Renaissance. Indeed it is possible that Scotland never fully recovered from that disaster. It was, wrote Francis Jeffrey, "the day that broke for ever the pride and splendour of the country."[7] In the present century, the film director John Grierson has said, "We were driven into the wilderness of national poverty at Flodden by the English and the English have never let us out of it to this day."[8]

The sorry record of destruction continued long after Flodden. In 1544, for example, Henry VIII sent the English fleet under the Earl of Hertford to sack and burn Leith, Edinburgh, Holyrood and all the towns and villages between them and Dunbar. In the following year, the same Earl of Hertford crossed the Border by land and destroyed 5 market towns, 243 villages, 16 fortified places, hundreds of churches and the abbeys of Kelso, Melrose, Dryburgh and Roxburgh. The ruins of these abbeys remain to this day, giving us some idea of how much was lost. But Henry VIII's intervention in Scotland was not confined to marauding armies. Like other English rulers before and since, he used both the stick and the carrot, or, to be more precise, the sword and the bribe. He continued the traditional English policy of seeking out disaffected, greedy or ambitious Scots who could be bribed to serve English interests. There was often, therefore, a faction in Scotland who were secretly in the pay of England. This became a particularly tempting policy to England at the time of the Reformation when the spread of the new religious ideas offered the prospect of breaking Scotland's historical alliance with France. Then, as later, it was not easy to unravel the complex interplay of self-interest and ideological conviction.

From the Reformation to the Enlightenment

The Reformation led to a fundamental change in Scotland's international alliances and in the relationship with England. To Protestant Scotland the continuation of the alliance with Catholic France became untenable. For the first time in more than 300 years, an element of mutual interest affected relations between England and Scotland and pressure towards co-operation instead of conflict began to be felt. So drastic a change did not come easily, but only after some two centuries of travail which culminated with the defeat of the Jacobites at Culloden in 1746. The sixteenth century, when this process began, was a time of quite extraordinary self-confidence in England which was rationalised and encouraged by theological writers like John Foxe and John Aylmer. They interpreted the Book of Revelation to prove, to their own satisfaction, that Elizabeth was a latter-day Constantine, destined as a Godly Prince to defeat the Anti-Christ and save and lead the world. Aylmer even proclaimed that "God is English". Scottish reformers taking refuge in England, and in particular John Knox, came under the influence of these curious ideas, in spite of the destruction of what passed as argument by Napier of Merchiston. The acceptance by the Kirk in Scotland of the Authorised Version of the Bible in 1611 reflected a new attitude to England. To generations of Scots it carried the implication that whether or not God was English, he certainly spoke English, and that it was the proper tongue for serious and weighty matters. Nothing could have done more to undermine the status of the Scots language at the time when it was beginning to evolve a prose to match its high achievement in verse.

In recent years, the Scottish Reformation has, on the whole, had a bad press, mainly because of its tendency to regard music, dance and the drama as frivolous distractions from the serious matter of man's relations with God. On the other hand, the Kirk has been a beneficial force in more than one direction. It embodies the Scottish egalitarian instinct and distrust of ranks and hierarchy in its representative structure of Kirk Sessions, Presbyteries, Synods and General Assembly. This was the first attempt in these islands to create democratic representation, open to all classes of the community, some 300 years before it was attempted in Parliament. Secondly, from the sixteenth century onwards, it placed high value on education and set about the task of establishing a free school in every parish. By the end of the following century, this policy had been so successful that the historian Thomas Babington Macaulay believed that it had made the common people in Scotland the most intelligent in Europe. "Scotland made such progress", he wrote, "in all that constitutes civilisation, as the old world had never seen equalled, and as even the new world has scarcely seen surpassed... This wonderful change is to be attributed, not indeed solely, but principally, to the national system of education."[9]

From its beginning, Calvinism has been an intellectual religion, elaborating its doctrines by a process of rigorous logic. This approach was followed not only by the theological writers but by every service in the Kirk. The emphasis was on a closely-argued sermon, which the congregation were expected both to follow and to subject to a critical analysis. In his novel *Rob Roy*, Walter Scott describes such a service in Glasgow Cathedral and he concludes:

> The Scotch, it is well known, are more remarkable for the exercise of their intellectual powers, than for the keeness of their feelings; they are, therefore, more moved by logic than by rhetoric, and more attracted by acute and argumentative reasoning on doctrinal points, than influenced by the enthusiastic appeals to the heart and to the passions, by which popular preachers in other countries win the favour of their hearers.[10]

Whether the Kirk created or responded to this national addiction to metaphysical speculation and logical argument, the fact is that for a long period most of the population were exposed to this sort of intellectual exercise every Sunday of their lives.

The parish schools produced a high level of literacy, probably higher than in any other country in Europe for about 300 years. The universities were in touch with the movements of European thought. The whole people were trained in "acute and argumentative reasoning" by the services of the Kirk. All these influences together prepared the way for the intellectual and artistic explosion of the eighteenth century. As John MacQueen has said, "The Scottish Enlightenment was the natural, almost the inevitable, outcome of several centuries of Scottish and European intellectual history."[11]

The change which the Reformation brought to the relationship with England was reinforced by a dynastic accident, the accession of a Scottish King, James VI, to the English throne in 1603. This was a consequence of the marriage of the daughter of Henry VII of England to James IV of Scotland. When it was under discussion in the English Court, some of Henry's advisers pointed to the risk that it might bring England under the rule of a Scottish prince. Henry told them not to worry. If that happened, it would mean the accession, not of England to Scotland, but of Scotland to England, since "the greater would always draw the less, as England had drawn Normandy under her sway."[12] He was right. The transfer of the royal court to London deprived Scotland at a stroke of the control of the executive, of state appointments and of the conduct of foreign policy. Royal patronage of the arts disappeared with the King. Scots was no longer the language of a royal court and inevitably began to lose the status of a national speech. In the words of Hume Brown, Scotland had become "a severed and a withered branch and her people knew it".

By the beginning of the eighteenth century, this position had become intolerable. The monarch was still much more than a constitutional myth, and in fact the effective head of executive government. Scotland was nominally independent, but was subject to a monarch who was under the strong influence of English ministers. Matters came to a head over the Darien Scheme, approved by William as King of Scotland, but undermined by him as King of England. The Scottish Parliament of 1703, largely under the inspiration of Andrew Fletcher of Saltoun, decided that it must either free policy and its execution from royal control or choose a separate successor to the throne of Scotland. The English response was to press for an incorporating union which would absorb the Scottish Parliament in the same way as the Scottish monarchy had been absorbed. This was achieved in 1707, in defiance of the wishes of the people of Scotland at large, by a mixture of bribery, propaganda and military intimidation.[13]

The Jacobite risings were in part an expression of hostility to the Union, but the issue was not simple and clear-cut. Part of the price which England had been prepared to pay for the Union was the acceptance, and indeed guarantee, of the Presbyterian Kirk in Scotland. A restoration of the Stuarts implied the revival of the French alliance and a threat to Presbyterianism. This was a dilemma which meant a painful choice between unpalatable alternatives. Scots might opt, in all conscience, for either side. There were therefore Scots in Cumberland's army at Culloden and some were involved in the barbarous oppression which he carried out in the Highlands after the battle. This, the first exercise of English power in Scotland after the Union, was an act of genocide, the deliberate suppression of a people, a way of life, a culture and a language.

From the earliest times, Scotland has been a multi-racial and a multilingual community. We have literatures in four languages, Gaelic, Latin, Scots and English. At the time of Culloden, Gaelic was spoken in more than half of the country and by about a third of the people. As a direct consequence of the policies imposed after Culloden, which made the Clearances possible, the Highlands are now largely uninhabited, and Gaelic has been driven to its last stronghold in the Western Isles. Perthshire, for instance, had a rich oral literature in poetry and story. With the loss of the language, the curtain falls and only scraps of the literature remain. In the words which Tacitus attributed to Calgacus, "They made a desert and they called it peace."

It was against this discouraging background that occurred the great efflorescence of the Scottish eighteenth century, a period of achievement in literature, science and the arts, for which you can find a parallel in a small country only in Periclean Athens or Renaissance Florence. Certainly, it was the culmination of a long process; so rich a growth can only spring from deep roots. Perhaps also, in a paradoxical way, the immediate political circumstances were a spur to effort. The humiliation of 1707 had threatened the extinction of Scotland. Now the intellect and the arts were being called in evidence to show that Scotland was not to be ignored. One aspect of this was a determination to find new life in the old literary roots. This was explicit in the anthologies of the older poetry, such as John Watson's *Choice Collection* of 1706 and Allan Ramsay's *The Ever Green* of 1724, which were among the first signs of revival. Like MacDiarmid in the present century, they went back to Dunbar as a preparation for a new advance. Burns collected songs and Scott the ballads in the same spirit of resistance to cultural assimilation. Ramsay, Fergusson and Burns wrote poetry in Scots with this conscious purpose, and all three strongly condemned the Union. Both Scott and Galt were anxious to record a Scottish way of life that was being eroded under pressure, and they used Scots as a necessary part of this. At the same time, and in the same spirit, there was a rich flowering of Gaelic poetry in the work of Alasdair Mac Mhaighstir Alasdair,

Donnachadh Ban, Rob Donn and Uilleam Ros.

On the other hand, the philosophers, historians, economists and sociologists, Hume, Robertson, Smith, Adam, Ferguson and the others, took pains to write in English but it was not the language which they spoke. An English visitor, Edward Topham, said of them: "They appear to me, from their conversation, to write English as a foreign tongue; their mode of talking, phrase and expression, but little resembling the language of their works."[14] They wrote English partly for the same reason that George Buchanan wrote Latin, to reach a wider audience. Also, they were faced with a difficult choice. As Ramsay of Ochtertyre explained it at the time, the events of the seventeenth century had frustrated the development of a Scots prose. In the following century, the literati had either to undertake what Ramsay called the "Herculean labour" of creating a prose suitable for their purposes or the only slightly less difficult task of learning to write English. "In this generous but unpromising attempt our countrymen at length succeeded, to the conviction of all the world."[15] To some extent, Ramsay was looking for an excuse. The need to find a workable prose does not explain the neurotic anxiety with which the literati excised every Scots word or turn of phrase and which provoked the old joke that Hume died confessing not his sins but his Scotticisms.

There was a parallel in the content of their writing. They were preoccupied with the evolution of human society. This was forced on their attention because they were living in Scotland at a time of particularly rapid and violent change, following the loss of independence, the destruction of Highland Society after the '45 and the beginning of the industrial revolution. But if their ideas evolved from their Scottish experience, there is remarkably little sign of it in their writing. Take the case of Adam Ferguson. He was a Gaelic-speaking Highlander, born in Logierait in Perthshire in 1724, and he spent nine years as chaplain to the Highland regiment, the Black Watch, immediately after Culloden. In one of his surviving letters, he makes it plain how much he admired the Highland way of life that was being destroyed in his own lifetime. But when he wrote about social change, and speculated about its causes and effects, he drew his examples from ancient Greece and Rome, or the Red Indians of North America or almost anywhere but Scotland. The same is true of most of his fellow literati. Perhaps the reality of the Scottish situation after the Union and Culloden was so painful that they had to disguise their thought in generalities.

Certainly, there were many other contributory factors. Everywhere in Europe education was still preoccupied with Latin, and to a lesser extent with Greek. It was natural to look to ancient Greece and Rome because their literature and history were more familiar to the educated than those of their own time and country. Sweeping generality was the fashion of the age. There were strong pressures on conformity with the ruling establishment because of their monopoly of patronage. The weight of the London market was already making itself felt. Both Hume and Smith found their publisher there, even if he was Scottish.

Also, there was another attitude which was more openly acknowledged in the second half of the eighteenth century than at any time before or since. Certain people in certain moods felt that they should make the best of a bad job and accept the political implications of the Union by resigning themselves to assimilation. It was a mood, especially acute after Culloden, of *let us forget the past and try to be English*. No doubt, there have been Scots then and subsequently who have followed this policy in practice, if not always in theory. They have always been a minority, although sometimes an influential one. They have remained a minority partly because of the resilience of the Scottish sense of identity and partly because of the attitude of the English themselves. There is a well-known letter in which David Hume (who was British Chargé d'Affaires in Paris at the time) replies to a suggestion of this sort. "Can you seriously talk of my continuing an Englishman? Am I, or are you, an Englishman? Will they allow us to be so? Do they not treat with Derision our Pretensions to that Name, and with Hatred our just Pretensions to surpass and to govern them?"[16]

Hume was more than half serious in talking about these pretensions. His letters are full of condemnation of the people whom he called "the Barbarians who inhabit the Banks of the Thames". "John Bull's prejudices are ridiculous", he remarked, "as his Insolence is intolerable." He wrote to Edward Gibbon to express polite surprise that an Englishman in that age could write a book of the quality of his *Decline and Fall of the Roman Empire*. The most frequently quoted passage of all from his letters is one where he salutes the achievements of the Scottish Enlightenment: "Really it is admirable how many Men of Genius this country produces at present. It is not strange that, at a time when we have lost our Princes, our Parliaments, our independent Government, even the Presence of our chief Nobility, are unhappy in our Accent and Pronunciation, speak a very corrupt Dialect of the Tongue which we make use of; is it not strange, I say, that, in these Circumstances, we shou'd really be the People most distinguish'd for Literature in Europe?"[17] Adam Smith takes a similar position in his explanation of the reasons for the superiority of the Scottish Universities over the English.[18] There is a significant remark in Adam Ferguson's Essay on the History of Civil Society. The whole book is an argument in favour of the social advantages of life in a community, and he says: "We need not enlarge our communities, in order to enjoy these advantages. We frequently obtain them in the most remarkable degree, where nations remain independent, and are of small extent."[19] Whatever the reason for the flight of the Scottish Enlightenment literati into generality, it was not due to an inferiority complex or a lack of concern for the interest, standing and reputation of Scotland.

It remains true that the literati in most of their public utterances moved in a disembodied world of pure intellect. One of the first to criticise them for this was John Gibson Lockhart in the book *Peter's Letters to His Kinsfolk*, published in 1819. He discusses the whole question in a letter about a visit to Walter Scott at Abbotsford. The literati of the previous century, he says, had displayed a force of intellect as applied to matters of reasoning, but had largely neglected both feeling and the resources of Scottish history and literature. "The folly of slighting and concealing what remains concealed within herself, is one of the worst and most pernicious that can beset a country, in the situation wherein Scotland stands." Scott, he added, was the great genius who had shown Scotland "her own national character as a mine of intellectual wealth, which remains in a great measure unexplored".[20]

No one who reads much of Scott can fail to see that one of the mainsprings of his being was a deep concern about the erosion of the Scottish identity and a determination to resist it by drawing on the resources of Scottish history and literature. You can see it in the Introduction to his first substantial work, *The Minstrelsy of the Scottish Border* (1802):

By such efforts, feeble as they are, I may contribute something to the history of my native country, the peculiar features of whose manners and character are daily melting and dissolving into those of her sister and ally. And, trivial as may appear such an offering to the Manes of a Kingdom, once proud and independent, I hang it upon her altar with a mixture of feeling which I shall not attempt to describe.

"There is no mistaking," as Edwin Muir said, "the emotion in these words."[21] You can see it again in an episode, which Lockhart recounts in his *Life*, after a meeting of the Faculty of Advocates in Edinburgh in 1806. They had been discussing proposals to bring the administration of justice in Scotland closer to English practice. Lockhart tells us that Scott opposed them with "a flow and energy of eloquence for which those who knew him best had been quite unprepared". He continues:

> When the meeting broke up, he walked across the Mound on his way to Castle Street, between Mr Jeffrey and another of his reforming friends, who complimented him on the rhetorical powers he had been displaying, and would willingly have treated the subject-matter of the discussion playfully. But his feeling had been moved to an extent far beyond their apprehension: he exclaimed, "No, no — 'tis no laughing matter; little by little, whatever your wishes may be, you will destroy and undermine, until nothing of what makes Scotland Scotland shall remain." And so saying, he turned round to conceal his agitation — but not until Mr Jeffrey saw tears gushing down his cheek — resting his head until he recovered himself on the wall of the Mound. Seldom, if ever, in his more advanced age, did any feelings obtain such mastery. [22]

These examples are from the beginning of Scott's career. The fullest statement of his feelings and opinions on these matters appeared towards the end of it in *The Letters of Malachi Malagrowther* of 1826. "I will sleep quieter in my grave," he told James Ballantyne, "for having so fair an opportunity of speaking my mind."[23] These *Letters* make a powerful case for the ideas that diversity is preferable to uniformity and centralisation; that Scottish characteristics are valuable for their own sake and should not be abandoned without good reason; that government should be responsive to local needs and wishes; that the overburdened government machine in London should refrain from interference in Scottish affairs. [24] "There has been in England a gradual and progressive system of assuming the management of affairs entirely and exclusively proper to Scotland, as if we were totally unworthy of having the management of our own concerns."[25] Scott's position on this matter is very close to views which are widely held in Scotland today; we have still not found a remedy to the problem which disturbed him so deeply. MacDiarmid has pointed out that the line of Scott's thought "leads naturally on to the separatist position".[26] Indeed, when it comes to the question of Scotland, there is much in common between Scott, the professed Tory, and MacDiarmid, the professed Communist.

One might ask why this issue first came to a head more than a hundred years after the Union. Scott's answer, and modern scholarship has confirmed that he was right, is that English interference began seriously only in the early nineteenth century. Before that, Scotland had been left to sink or swim by her own devices, with the disastrous exception of the suppression of the Highlands after the '45. When James Stuart Mackenzie was appointed in 1761 as the Minister responsible for Scotland, he was surprised to find no papers in his office and no sign that any business was being carried on.[27] Of course, at that time, and for long afterwards, the role of government was very limited. Education and such social services as existed were the concern not of the State, but of the Kirk and the burghs. The Union had left the Scottish legal system, the church and local government intact. They continued to function in their separate ways, although deprived of a Parliament which could explore abuses and seek reforms. In Scott's words, Scotland had been left "under the guardianship of her own institutions, to win her silent way to national wealth and consequence... But neglected as she was, and perhaps because she was neglected, Scotland, reckoning her progress during the space from the close of the American war to the present day, has increased her prosperity in a ratio more than five times greater than that of her more fortunate and richer sister. She is now worth the attention of the learned faculty, and God knows she has plenty of it... A spirit of proselytism has of late shown itself in England for extending the benefits of their system, in all its strength and weakness, to a country, which has been hitherto flourishing and contented under its own. They adopted the conclusion, that all English enactments are right; but the system of municipal law in Scotland is not English, therefore it is wrong."[28]

The Nineteenth Century Decline

Scotland in the early nineteenth century, when the Elephant began to assert itself, was "flourishing and contented" in more than a material sense. Her universities were still a major source of stimulation and new ideas for the whole world. The ministers of the Kirk had produced in the *Statistical Account* the first attempt anywhere to study conditions of a country in depth as a rational basis for future policy, even if Scotland had no parliament to give legislative effect to the ideas. Literature was more flourishing in Scotland than almost anywhere else. Scott was the dominant figure internationally, but he was not alone. Both Galt and Hogg were innovative but rooted in the Scottish tradition. *Blackwood's Magazine* and the *Edinburgh Review* were among the most influential periodicals in the world. The Edinburgh of the time was described by John Buchan in these words:

> Many of the great academic figures had gone, but Dugald Stewart and John Playfair were alive; there was a national school of science and philosophy as well of letters, and there were scholarly country gentlemen, like Clerk of Eldin and Sir William Forbes, to make a bridge between learning and society. Edinburgh was a true capital, a clearing house for the world's culture and a jealous repository of Scottish tradition."[29]

Lord Cockburn, the most perceptive observer of the contemporary scene, described this period as "the last purely Scotch age that Scotland was destined to see". "According to the modern rate of travelling," he continued (he was writing in 1852), "the capitals of Scotland and of England were then about 2400 miles asunder. Edinburgh was still more distant in its style and habits. It had then its own independent tastes, and ideas, and pursuits."[30]

Already by 1852, Cockburn remarked on a sudden and drastic change. The whole country had begun to be "absorbed in the ocean of London". Edinburgh, to some extent, resisted. "This city has advantages, including its being the capital of Scotland, its old reputation, and its external beauties, which have enabled it, in a certain degree, to resist the centralising tendency, and hitherto always supplied it with a succession of eminent men. But, now that London is at our door, how precarious is our hold of them, and how many have we lost."[31] In his *Journal*, some twenty years earlier, Scott had already remarked on the beginning of the same process: "In London, there is a rapid increase of business and its opportunities. Thus London licks the butter off our bread, by opening a better market for ambition. Were it not for the difference of the religion and laws, poor Scotland could hardly keep a man that is worth having."[32] "Triumphant and eclipsing England", wrote Lockhart, "like an immense magnet, absolutely draws the needles from the smaller ones."[33]

We might take Carlyle's departure for London in 1834 as the symbolic date of this abrupt and astonishing loss of self-confidence and achievement. For about 100 years Scotland, and Edinburgh in particular, had been in a ferment of artistic and intellectual activity. It was a veritable renaissance which had profound effects on the evolution of the modern world. Both in its sources and its consequences it was international, but it was sustained by Scottish tradition and it was not dominated by any one external influence. A generation earlier, it would have been natural for Carlyle to stay in Scotland and participate in the intellectual excitement. By 1834, the interference of London in Scottish affairs, aided by the improved communications with railways and steamships, made it equally natural for him and countless others to succumb to the pull of the "immense magnet". "The operation of the commercial principle which tempts all superiority to try its fortune in the greatest accessible market, is perhaps irresistible," wrote Cockburn, "but anything is surely to be lamented which annihilates local intellect, and degrades the provincial spheres which intellect and its consequences can alone adorn."[34] This is precisely what happened. Scott, writing in 1826, had described the English pressure as beginning in "the last fifteen or twenty years, and more especially the last ten".[35] Within two or three decades, the pull and the pressure (for it worked both ways) threatened to reduce Scotland to provincial mediocrity.

The effect was most obvious in literature, which is, I suppose, as good an indication as any of the cultural health of a society. After the brilliance of Scott, Galt and Hogg, all of whom died in the 1830s, there is a melancholy hiatus for the next fifty years. Scotland, which had shown the way at the beginning, failed to continue the development of the realistic novel which distinguished the literatures of England, France and Russia in the mid-nineteenth century. There was, to use a phrase of George Davie's, a sorry "failure of intellectual nerve".[36] William Power's explanation is that Scottish writers had "lost the native tradition, the literary sense of Scottishness. They floundered about in the English scheme of things, and never caught on to anything vital".[37] Gaelic poetry suffered a similar decline. The sensitivity, intelligence and virtuosity of the eighteenth century was followed by a collapse into triviality in the nineteenth. In one of his letters, Scott said: "If you *unscotch* us, you will make us damned mischievous Englishmen."[38] Not so much mischievous, perhaps, as inadequate and second-rate.

An even more astonishing, and, one might think, impertinent campaign of anglicisation was directed against the most successful of Scottish institutions, the universities. They were, after all, the powerhouse of new ideas and of trained minds which had made the Scottish Enlightenment. They were respected, admired and imitated throughout the civilised world, except perhaps in England with its customary attitude of complacent insularity. At the same period, the two universities in England itself were sunk in lethargy, "steeped in port and prejudice", as Edward Gibbon expressed it.[39] Yet, from early in the nineteenth century, there was a determined and ultimately largely successful campaign to subordinate the Scottish universities to English standards. This whole subject is the theme of George Davie's classic book, *The Democratic Intellect*, one of the most important written in Scotland this century. It was, he wrote, "the tortuous, dark revolution whereby a nation noted educationally both for social mobility and for fixity of first principle gradually reconciled itself to an alien system in which principles traditionally did not matter and a rigid social immobilism was the accepted thing." The intention was "to prepare the way for the cultural subordination of Scotland to England parallel to its political subordination."[40] Significantly, the first move in this campaign was in 1826, the year in which Scott wrote *The Letters of Malachi Malagrowther*.

Shortly after the publication of George Davie's book in 1961, C.P. Snow, who wrote one of the most enthusiastic reviews of it, made a speech in Edinburgh. He summed up the matter in these words:

150 years ago Edinburgh had probably the best University in the world, with a deep and serious intellectual tradition, which still exists in this country. I could wish that Scottish education had remained a little more

different from English rather than the reverse, because the Scots have always believed in democratic education and in the generalised intellect in a way that my more empirical countrymen have never quite believed.[41]

Another distinguished Englishman, V. H. Galbaith, was for many years Professor of British History in Edinburgh. When he left in 1944, he drew conclusions from his experiences in Scotland: "I am perfectly sure that the future of Scotland lies in a tremendous development of its own affairs, and having the power to do that. No proposal with regard to education which comes up here from England is worth a damn to you."[42] Unfortunately, this was not the view which had prevailed during the previous hundred years.

A similar process applied to the schools, again in spite of their acknowledged achievement. As in the universities, the school system was distorted in the course of the nineteenth century by the imposition of incompatible English ideas. One of the qualities of Scottish education from the sixteenth century was its accessibility to the whole population without distinction of social class. Take, for example, the High School of Edinburgh, described by James Grant as "the most important in Scotland and intimately connected with the literature and progress of the Kingdom."[43] In a speech in 1825 Lord Brougham said this about it: "A school like the old High School of Edinburgh is invaluable, and for what is this so? It is because men of the highest and lowest rank of society send their children to be educated together."[44] Yet at about the time he was saying this, it was becoming increasingly common for the aristocracy and the more socially ambitious of the middle class to send their sons to the so-called public schools in England which were run on the opposite principle of social exclusivity. For those who wanted to compromise, or who could not afford Eton or the rest, a number of schools on the English model began to be established in Scotland, beginning with the Edinburgh Academy in 1824. Apart from the social implications, there was a fundamental divergence in intellectual approach because the English, or imitation-English, schools believed in early specialisation in place of the Scottish principle of a general, broadly based education. The effect of all of this was socially divisive and it tended to create an influential class whose education, and therefore attitudes and allegiance, were more English that Scottish. They were predisposed to form an internal lobby favourably inclined towards anglicisation.

Even so, it is puzzling that the country succumbed so easily when it had such solid achievement behind it and such a history of determined resistance. There were a number of reasons, some peculiar to the period and some which have persisted. In the first place, the assertion of English influence in the early nineteenth century was contemporary with the victory over Napoleon. It was the beginning of a period, which lasted about 100 years, when Britain (which means predominantly England) was the richest and most successful of World Powers. It was the zenith of the British Empire which coloured a large part of the map of the world in red. England was in a triumphant and assertive mood and more than usually difficult to resist. The Napoleonic Wars had direct effects on Scotland. They caused the Establishment, either reacting in panic or seizing an opportunity, to suppress radicalism and curb the free expression of political ideas. At the same time, they encouraged a spirit of British patriotism which tended to displace or conceal traditional Scottish attitudes.

The development of the Empire was to a disproportionate extent the work of Scots who were active everywhere as explorers, administrators, engineers, soldiers, doctors, missionaries and teachers. This preoccupation with careers in the Empire strongly contributed to the distortion of Scottish education. When entrance examinations for the overseas services were introduced, they were based on the English educational system and the Scottish schools and universities had to adjust accordingly if their candidates were to have a fair chance. This helped to establish a habit of concentration on English history and literature to the exclusion of the Scottish which still persists much to the detriment of Scottish self-knowledge and self-confidence. It may well be true, as Elizabeth Hay wrote recently, that "the Scots participated in the Empire as Scots. They did not feel it was England's Empire ... They thought of themselves as Scottish first and then British."[45] Even so, the energy which the Scots expended in India, Canada, Australia, New Zealand and Africa was lost to Scotland. The one benefit, if it was a benefit, which the Union brought to Scotland was access to careers in the Empire while it lasted. In any case, it was benefit to individuals, not to Scotland as a whole. When this loss of population is added to the wholesale clearance of the Highlands and the emigration compelled by the neglect of Scotland itself, it amounts to a massive haemorrhage of talent, energy and skill. This has been on a scale which threatens the very survival of Scotland; but Scotland had no Parliament even to discuss the matter and no government to take action. The haemorrhage has continued. Writing in 1935, Edwin Muir drew the obvious conclusion:

> Scotland is gradually being emptied of its population, its spirit, its wealth,
> industry, art, intellect, and innate character... If a country exports its most
> enterprising spirits and best minds year after year, for fifty or a hundred
> or two hundred years, some result will inevitably follow... (Scotland is) a
> country which is becoming lost to history. [46]

In the early nineteenth century the people of Scotland were even more
defenceless than they are today. Not only was there no Scottish parliament,
but only an insignificant part of the population had the right to vote for the
small minority of Scottish members in the British House. Parliamentary
Reform began in 1832, but it was not until the Third Reform Act of 1884
that most adult men,but still no women, had the vote. It was only then that
there began to be any real opportunity for the people at large to have any
influence on events. It is probably not coincidental that it was at about the
same time, as we shall see, that some restraint began to be applied to the
nineteenth-century decline.

On the other hand, if Scotland had no Parliament, it did have the long-
established democratic structure of the Church of Scotland, several centuries
in advance of Parliament in accepting the democratic ideal of equality.
Although the General Assembly did not have the political power of a
Legislature, the Church was a great cohesive force in Scottish Society. It
had far more impact on the lives of the people than the remote Government
in London, especially as it was largely responsible for the social services.
In Scott's phrase, it was one of the "institutions" which carried on the life of
the country after it was deprived of its Parliament in 1707. As it happened,
the Church was incapacitated by an internal crisis precisely at the time when
English interference began to assert itself and at the same time as the existing
social structure was under strain because of the effects of the new
industrialisation. The crisis was a consequence of the imposition of the
system of patronage on the Church by Parliament, although this violated
guarantees contained in the Union settlement itself. By 1843, this led to the
remarkable event of the Disruption, when 450 ministers of the Church, more
than a third of the total, gave up their churches, homes and incomes for the
sake of their conscience. It was, Cockburn wrote, "as extraordinary, and in
its consequences will probably prove as permanent as any single transaction

in the history of Scotland, the Union alone excepted... It is one of the rarest occurrences in moral history. I know of no parallel to it."[47] Eventually the Church for the most part reunited, but it never regained the pivotal position which it had held in the life of the country before the Disruption. Nothing has, so far, taken its place. Scotland as never before was left, in Edwin Muir's phrase, with "no centre, no heart radiating a living influence."[48] It is a vacuum which in modern conditions only a Parliament can fill.

For all these reasons, Scotland was particularly vulnerable to anglicisation when the process began effectively in the early nineteenth century. The most systematic study of it so far has been one by an American sociologist, Michael Hechter, in his book *Internal Colonialism*, first published in 1975. He identifies three characteristics:

1. A defining characteristic of imperial expansion is that the centre must disparage the indigenous culture of peripheral groups.

2. One of the consequences of this denigration of indigenous culture is to undermine the native's will to resist the colonial regime.

[I might remark in passing that one of the commonest forms of this denigration is to describe anything Scottish as "parochial" or "narrowly nationalist", and this is usually said by someone who is himself particularly parochial and chauvinist.]

3. Political incorporation also had a decisive effect on the progress of anglicisation, which proceeded not only by government fiat, but through the voluntary assimilation of peripheral élites.[49]

The implications of Hechter's analysis is that this process, which also applied to Wales and Ireland, was the result of a deliberate and sustained government policy. At least as far as Scotland is concerned, I do not think that this is normally true. English policy in this respect has usually been unconscious, except in moments of panic, as in 1745 and the 1970s. It has been the result more of ignorance and indifference towards Scottish interests and aspirations than of a conscious plan to thwart them. In R. L. Stevenson's words, "The egoism of the Englishman is self-contained. He does not seek to proselytise. He takes no interest in Scotland or the Scots, and, what is the

unkindest cut of all, he does not care to justify his indifference."[50] The
sheer elephantine weight of greater numbers and wealth, and a majority of
about ten to one in Parliament, has applied itself without conscious effort.
The assumption, as Scott said in the *Malachi* letters, has always been that
what is English is right and what is not English is therefore wrong.

On the other hand, the efforts of those that Hechter calls the "peripheral
élite," the internal anglicisers, have often been deliberate and even
painstaking. In Hechter's words, "The conscious rationale behind
anglicisation among the peripheral élite was to dissociate themselves as
much as possible from the mass of their countrymen, who were so strongly
deprecated by the English culture. Thus, they eagerly learned to speak
English in the home, to emulate English manners and attitudes, to style
their very lives on the English model. In effect, this was a voluntary
renunciation of their national origins."[51] This is a phenomenon which began
with a small minority as long ago as the Union of the Crowns in 1603.
When the King and Court moved to London, the politically and socially
ambitious inevitably followed and had to adopt English speech and fashions
if they were to be found acceptable. After 1707, Scottish members of
Parliament had to do the same to avoid the mockery of the House of
Commons. Careers in government service had the same effect. We have
already noted the influence of this on the Scottish educational system which
in consequence itself tended to become an instrument of anglicisation. To
this were added in more recent times the forces of the London press and,
even more powerfully, of radio and television. By these means, and once
again largely unconsciously on their part, generations of Scots have been
brought up to regard English traditions and habits of thought and expression
as the norm and to be left almost entirely in ignorance of their own. It is
easy to see why Muir felt that Scotland was "a country which is becoming
lost to history."

Does it Matter?

Are we then an endangered species, about to become in fact, as some people already regard us, no more than the inhabitants of a region of England? If so, does it matter? Should we perhaps yield to superior force and give up the struggle? I think that the answer to all of these questions depends on whether there is anything of value in the Scottish tradition which is worth an effort to preserve.

There is first of all the consideration that diversity has a value in itself and is to be preferred to uniformity, especially when it is imposed by external circumstances. This is a proposition to which most people would, I suppose, subscribe. A world reduced to uniformity would not only be dull, but also sterile; inventiveness and the arts would be stifled. Most of us would, as it were, be thinking in translation and trying to adopt attitudes which are not natural to us. Imitation is always likely to be inferior to the spontaneous. As Scott said in the *Malachi* letters:

> For God's sake, sir, let us remain as Nature made us, Englishmen, Irishmen, and Scotchmen, with something like the impress of our several countries upon each! We would not become better subjects, or more valuable members of the common empire, if we all resembled each other like so many smooth shillings. Let us love and cherish each other's virtues — bear with each other's failings — be tender to each other's prejudices — be scrupulously regardful of each other's rights. Lastly, let us borrow each other's improvements, but never before they are needed and demanded. The degree of national diversity between different countries is but an instance of that general variety which Nature seems to have adopted as a principle through all her works, as anxious, apparently, to avoid, as modern statesmen to enforce, anything like an approach to absolute uniformity.[52]

T. S. Eliot, consciously or unconsciously echoing Scott, argued, "It is to the advantage of England that the Welsh should be Welsh, the Scots Scots and the Irish Irish... It is an essential part of my case, that if the other cultures of the British Isles were wholly superseded by English culture, English culture would disappear too."[53] And the principle, of course, has a much wider application than to the British Isles alone.

The world as a whole has never had more need to defend its diversity than today. The forces working towards a monotonous uniformity have never been stronger in mass consumerism, mass advertising and mass entertainment. The rich diversity of human cultures is threatened by a stifling overlay of a meretricious appeal to the lowest common denominator. Pop music is its most obvious and appropriate symbol with its monotonous repetition and trite lyrics expressed in mock American speech, regardless of the natural language of the singer or his audience. It is in the interest of mankind as a whole that each of us should preserve our identity from the flood which threatens to engulf all of us. The Scottish struggle is part of a world struggle.

In Scotland we have had long experience of the consequences of the imposition through the schools and social pressures of external cultural standards. For over 200 years our schools have tried to suppress natural speech, Gaelic or Scots, and make their pupils ape the English. They have diverted attention from our own history, literature and achievements to those of England. The consequence has been a loss of articulacy, spontaneity and self-confidence. If a child is taught to be ashamed of his natural speech, he tends to lose all confidence in self-expression. If he is made to believe that everything of importance happened somewhere else, he is led towards an inferiority complex and a feeling of hopelessness and despair. It is a recipe for an unhealthy society, conditioned to failure, where the only hope is the escape of emigration.

That anything like this should happen in Scotland is particularly remarkable and outrageous in view of the extraordinary record of Scottish achievement. In the words of an American, Harold Orel: "The record is rich, when seen as an entirety, almost unbelievably so. No nation of its size has contributed as much to world culture."[54]

Another American, H. W. Thompson, in discussing the Scotland of the Enlightenment in the lifetime of Henry Mackenzie, concluded: "To discover comparable achievements by so small a nation in so short a time we should need to go back from the Age of Mackenzie to the Age of Pericles."[55] Yet another American, John Kenneth Galbraith, said that "the only serious rivals to the Scots were the Jews."[56] These comparisons are not exaggerated. "The peculiar history of the Scots," wrote Christopher Harvie, "has meant that, man for man, they have probably done more to create the modern world than any other nation."[57] Watt's improvements of the steam engine created the first Industrial Revolution. Clerk Maxwell's discoveries ushered in the new revolution of electronics. The modern approach to such diverse matters as history, economics, sociology, geology, chemistry, medicine and banking were all fundamentally affected by the Scottish Enlightenment. We have produced a notable literature in four languages, including much of the greatest poetry of the late Middle Ages. Our traditional song, poetry and dance are among the most vigorous to be found anywhere. Scots have made a remarkable contribution to many European countries as well as to those of the former British Empire all over the world. You would expect us all to agree with the judgement of the English historian, J. A. Froude: "No nation in Europe can look with more just pride on their past than the Scots, and no young Scotchman [and I would add woman, of course] ought to grow up in ignorance of what that past had been."[58] The anglicisation of our education has decreed otherwise. Ironically, at the same time, there is increasing appreciation of the Scottish contribution to our common civilisation in other countries from America to Japan.

It would be a particularly unfortunate loss of a component of human diversity if the Scottish approach to life were supplanted by the English because they are so fundamentally different, socially and intellectually. We share with the French — and perhaps this is the reason for the remarkable persistence of the spirit of the Auld Alliance — a fondness for first principles and an appreciation of precision and logic. The English distrust these things and make a virtue of acting by instinct without a rigorous, and perhaps inhibiting, intellectual analysis. The formidable English historian, H. T. Buckle, one of the great Victorians, made a deep study of this question as part of his preparation for his *History of Civilisation*. He concluded that there was:

> an essential antagonism which still exists between the Scotch and English minds; an antagonism extremely remarkable, when found among nations, both of whom, besides being contiguous, and constantly mixing together, speak the same language, read the same books, belong to the same empire,

and possess the same interests, and yet are, in many important respects, as different, as if there had never been any means of their influencing each other and as if they had never had anything in common.[59]

It is not, of course, a question of the superiority of one national tradition over another. All have their strengths and weaknesses; but the more diverse they are, the more likely they are to enrich our common civilisation with a wide range of achievement and offer a choice of different possible solutions to our problems. It is an impoverishment of civilisation as a whole, if a valuable national tradition is suppressed or supplanted by another. At the same time, the cross-fertilisation of ideas and influence is a fruitful source of stimulation, provided the recipient is free to take, in Scott's words, what is "needed and demanded", and to reject what is not suitable for his purposes. The stifling imposition by force or elephantine weight of alien standards, attitudes and values from one particular source is another matter.

The great mediaeval poetry of Scotland and the Scottish Enlightenment are examples of the benefits of wide international influence. The collapse of confidence and achievement after about 1830 is an example of the consequences of elephantine pressure.

Eric Linklater in, *The Lion and the Unicorn* 1935 summed up the effects of the substitution of English culture for "that diversity of cultures with which, in earlier times, Scotland had always been in contact":

By reason of its association with England, Scotland became insular. Its political frontier was broken down and its mind was walled up. Geographical or political enlargement, beyond certain limits, is nearly always accompanied by intellectual shrinkage.[60]

Revival

In *The Democratic Intellect* George Davie says that in the Scotland of the nineteenth century, "the old confident grip on the situation was noticeably slackening. Instead of the steady rhythm of independent institutional life, a new pattern emerged of alternation between catastrophe and renaissance, in which the distinctive national inheritance was more than once brought to the very brink of ruin only to be saved at the last minute by a sudden burst of reviving energy."[61] In the mid-nineteenth century, Scotland seemed about to decline into passive acceptance of provincial mediocrity, into what C. J. Watson has described as "the sense of weariness, of the absence of hope, and lacerating self-contempt which is a marked component in the psyche of colonised peoples".[62]

Even so, the decline was only in comparison to the generation before. There was strong resilience in the Scottish spirit in spite of the conformity on the surface. In Scotland, oral and traditional literature has always nourished and been nourished by literature of the more formal kind, as in the revival introduced by Watson and Ramsay in the eighteenth century. These traditions remained vigorously alive. In the mid-century, J. F. Campbell collected four volumes of Gaelic traditional stories. Towards the end of the century, Gavin Greig and the Rev. James Duncan found about 3,000 Scots songs alive in folk tradition in Buchan alone. William MacTaggart was painting from about the middle of the century. Brewster, Kelvin and Clerk Maxwell continued the scientific traditions of the Enlightenment, although they were no longer sustained by the "independent institutional life" which had encouraged the achievements of the previous century.

The first coherent "burst of reviving energy" came in the 1880s and 1890s. In this, as subsequently, political developments and the formation of new institutions coincided with a resurgence of literature and the other arts. It seems that a quickening of one aspect of Scottish life stimulates the others. In the 1880s, for instance, the Scottish Home Rule Association was formed and the conference of the Scottish Liberal Party adopted for the first time the policy of Home Rule for Scotland. Parliament passed an Act to re-establish the office of Secretary of State. The National Portrait Gallery, the Scottish Text Society and the Scottish History Society were formed. Stevenson wrote *Kidnapped* and *The Master of Ballantrae*. By 1895 Sir Patrick Geddes was able to write in his periodical, *Evergreen*, of a Scots Renaissance, long before the term was applied to the movement associated with Hugh MacDiarmid.

Geddes was himself a leader in this revival, devoted to the cause of escaping from the "intellectual thraldom of London" and restoring the old sympathies between Scotland and the Continent.[63] In the same spirit, he tried to found a College des Ecossais in Montpellier as a revival of the Scots College in Paris, established in 1326 as the first Scottish institution of higher learning.

The First World War intervened, with the destructive effects on Scottish communities chronicled by Lewis Grassic Gibbon in *Sunset Song*. Like the Napoleonic Wars, it diverted attention away from Scotland's own concerns. On the other hand, it purported to be a war fought for the right of self-determination and it did lead to the restoration of several small nations to the map of Europe. These ideas contributed to a second wave of "reviving energy" in the 1920s and 30s. This is associated particularly with Hugh MacDiarmid who campaigned throughout his life for Scottish independence and for a revival, not only of Scots and Gaelic, but of Scottish culture in the widest sense, far-ranging both in intellectual content and in its international ramifications. His work resumes and restates many of the constant themes of Scottish writing. In resisting anglicisation, he was echoing Scott; in returning to Dunbar for inspiration and example, he was following the lead of Ramsay; in extending the use of Scots, he was building on the foundation of Fergusson and Burns; in responding to the latest tendencies in international thought, and regarding all knowledge as an interlocking whole, he was in the tradition of the Scottish Enlightenment; in his radical politics he was extending a tradition that goes back through MacLean, Muir of Huntershill, the Covenanters, the Reformation and George Buchanan to the Declaration of Arbroath. "To MacDiarmid," wrote Tom Scott, "the English Ascendancy was a historical iniquity with no right but might behind it, and to be overthrown by all good men and true."[64]

Once again, literary, political and institutional developments moved forward together. MacDiarmid published *A Drunk Man Looks at the Thistle* in 1926. He became the centre of a very lively literary life, with poets, novelists and dramatists like Sydney Goodsir Smith, Robert Garioch, Sorley MacLean, George Campbell Hay, Neil Gunn, Lewis Grassic Gibbon, Eric Linklater, Robert Kemp, Robert Maclellan and many others. The National Library of Scotland was established in 1925 on the basis of the Advocates' Library, founded in 1680. (Like the National Portrait Gallery, this was made possible by private generosity). In 1936, the Saltire Society was formed to "work for a revival of the intellectual and artistic life of Scotland such as we experienced in the eighteenth century." The Scottish National Party was founded in 1934 by the fusion of two older parties. In 1939, the Government moved Departments concerned with Scotland from London to Edinburgh.

Again, a World War deferred expectations and scattered the men involved in the new atmosphere of intellectual vitality. However, during the War itself, MacDiarmid and the others continued to write and plan and work for the future. Tom Johnston as Secretary of State gave an impetus to the search for Scottish solutions to Scottish problems. The Scottish Convention began a campaign which led in 1949 to the collection of some two million signatures to a Covenant demanding a Scottish Parliament. In the immediate post-war period, both the political and the intellectual movements gathered momentum. The first Edinburgh International Festival was held in 1947. In the same year, the Scottish Arts Council became largely autonomous (although constitutionally still a part of the Arts Council of Great Britain). Since then it has been a valuable channel of public subsidy to the arts, and has contributed substantially to the revival of Scottish publishing and to the emergence of a diversity of literary magazines. Scottish historical scholarship in particular has acquired new vitality and challenged many accepted ideas of the Scottish past. The electoral successes of the SNP in the 1960s and 70s attracted attention as never before to Scottish issues. All political parties committed themselves to a measure of Scottish self-government. When the Scotland Act was put to the people in the Referendum of 1979, however, the Conservative Party campaigned for a "No" vote with the promise that they would introduce an improved measure with stronger powers. They then used the small "Yes" majority as a justification for taking no further action.

The optimism and self-confidence generated by the hopes of constitutional advance in the 1970s led to a marked quickening of the national life. There was an injection of new spirit into the Scottish theatre and a strong increase in the writing and publication of serious Scottish books. Planning for a revitalised Scotland was very active. The Saltire Society, for example, held a conference in 1977 to consider the policies necessary in an autonomous Scotland for the encouragement of artistic and intellectual life. The conference decided to consult all organisations concerned with these matters with a view to the formation of a combined think-tank. This, the Advisory Council for the Arts in Scotland, was established after wide consultation in 1981, two years after the Referendum.

This continuation of effort in spite of the setback was not untypical. There is no doubt that the muted "Yes" majority in the Referendum, and the confusion of the issues by the disingenuousness of the "No" campaign, brought with it a mood of humiliation and resignation. At the same time, the forward momentum was not entirely lost, even if much of it went below the surface. All political parties, with the present exception of the Conservatives, are more fully committed than ever to self-government, and these parties had more than 70% of the Scottish vote in the last two general elections. The Campaign for a Scottish Assembly has been active in promoting co-operation between the parties and in drawing up detailed plans for a Constitutional Convention. Constitutional advance now sems only a matter of time, but there is not much time left before it is too late.

This consideration of contemporary politics is unavoidable because it is central to the issue. In Donald Dewar's words, "There is a real connection between political power and the survival of a culture."[65] The close association which we have noted between political and cultural confidence and activity is not accidental. They have advanced together and declined together. Scotland is threatened with extinction as an active creative component of European civilisation because of the vacuum at its heart, the absence of any focus for the national life and the denial of responsibility for its own affairs. "I believe," said Eric Linklater, "that people degenerate when they lose control of their own affairs, and as a corollary, that resumption of control may induce regeneration. To any nation the essential vitamin is responsibility."[66]

Scotland is now poised for a new surge of political and cultural advance. It has been a slow process, but each of the surges during the last 100 years has left us a little further up the beach. We are equipped as never before with the tools for an intelligent understanding of our position, both in the results of the new historical scholarship and in such reference works as the *Companions* of David Daiches, Derek Thomson and Trevor Royle. W. L. Lorimer's *Translation of the New Testament* has given new force to Scottish prose. *The Concise Scots Dictionary* has made widely available the great resources of *The Scottish National Dictionary* and *The Dictionary of the Older Scottish Tongue*. The Report in 1985 of the Consultative Committee on the Curriculum was a positive revolution in the thought of Scottish educationalists. Their recommendation that "the Scottish dimension, Scottish language, literature, geography and history are not frills, but should be central to the education of the children who attend Scottish schools"[67] may seem self-evident but it is far from the practice which has prevailed up to the present. At the same time, there has probably never been a stronger political consensus on the need for constitutional change. As I write, the latest opinion poll on the subject shows a majority in favour of an independent Parliament. That is what we need. Any degree of self-government would be beneficial; but for Scotland to be free to develop and play its full part in Europe as in the past, it needs as much independence as Luxembourg or Denmark or any other member of the EEC.

Can we then be optimistic? Are we to be saved at the eleventh hour by another "burst of reviving energy"? Only, I think, if we all make a determined effort. All the positive forces which I have mentioned are opposed, if largely unconsciously, by the forces of assimilation and they have the weight of superior numbers and wealth on their side. Our minds are flooded daily by television programmes and very few of them originate in Scotland. To the activities of the internal anglicisers, who are always with us, are added an increasing number of immigrants who actually are English. This is a new phenomenon on anything like the present scale. We welcome them, as is proper, with our traditional hospitality. Many of them take trouble to learn about us and bring with them qualities of real value. Others live in a cocoon of deliberate and complacent ignorance of the society that surrounds them. This would not matter very much, except that many of them occupy key position in our institutions, even in those which are supposed to be the custodians of our traditions and values. This is prevalent not only in Government but in the universities, the theatre and even in local arts festivals where there is often no Scottish element at all. We are sometimes left feeling like strangers in our own country who are gradually being displaced by a colonial regime. It was such a thought as this that led James Campbell to say of the Clearances in his book, *Invisible Country*, in 1984: "Throughout the entire country there is the sense that what took place in the Highlands during the earlier part of last century is a clue to what has happened to modern Scotland."[68]

One of the founding members of the Saltire Society, Andrew Dewar Gibb, in considering the consequences of the elephantine pressures, concluded: "Thus have closer ties with England resulted in the debasement, if not the total destruction, of a great national possession."[69] When you consider the facts, this is a conclusion which it is difficult to avoid. As I have said, I do not think that this effect has been deliberate or malevolent, at least since the suppression of the Highland way of life; but it is inherent in the present constitutional position. We want to have friendly and productive relationships with all countries, and certainly with our nearest neighbour. Not the least of the reasons why we urgently need a constitutional change is that otherwise an equitable and fair relationship with England is impossible.

Postscript

In Bed with an Elephant was written in 1985. Since then there has been another, and I hope decisive, "burst of reviving energy". This was displayed most prominently, but not only, in the decisive result of the Referendum of 11 September 1997. I said in 1985 that Scotland was poised for a new political and cultural advance; I am glad that my confidence was not misplaced.

There is one point which should be brought up to date. Since 1994 the Scottish Arts Council is no longer a part of the Arts Council of Great Britain (which no longer exists), but is autonomous and directly responsible to the Scottish Office.

P.H.S.
June 1998

References

1   Henry Thomas Buckle, "On Scotland and the Scotch Intellect", in
    History of Civilisation in England (1857, 1861) J Hanham
    (Chicago 1970) p31.
2   James Anthony Froude, *History of England from the Fall of
    Wolsey to the Defeat of the Spanish Armada* (London 1873) iv p5.
3   The Declaration of Arbroath, *ed.* Sir James Fergusson (Edinburgh
    1970) p9.
4   *The Letters of Robert Burns, ed*. J de Lancey Ferguson (Oxford
    1931) i p106: letter to Dr John Moore, 2 August 1787.
5   John Hill Burton, *The Scot Abroad* (Edinburgh 1881) pp364-5.
6   Dugald Stewart, *Collected Works, ed*. Sir William Hamilton
    (Edinburgh 1884), i p551.
7   Francis Jeffrey, review of Scott's *Marmion, Edinburgh Review*
    (April 1808).
8   John Grierson, "The Salt of the Earth", in *John Grierson's Scotland,
    ed*. Forsyth Hardy (Edinburgh 1979), p33.
9   Thomas Babington Macaulay, *History of England* (London 1858),
    iv p782-3
10 Sir Walter Scott, *Rob Roy* ch.20
11 John MacQueen, *Progress and Poetry: The Enlightenment and
    Scottish Literature*, (Edinburgh 1982) p5.
12 *Quoted in* R L Mackie, *King James IV of Scotland* (Edinburgh
    1958) p93.
13 This is discussed in my *1707: The Union of Scotland and England*
    (Edinburgh 1979 and 1994), especially ch.7.
14 Edward Topham, *Letters from Edinburgh 1774-5* (London 1776,
    Facsimile Edition Edinburgh 1971), p55.
15 John Ramsay of Ochtertyre, *Scotland and Scotsmen in the
    Eighteenth Century, ed*. A A Allardyce (Edinburgh and London
    1888), i p9.
16 *The Letters of David Hume, ed.* J Y T Greig (Oxford 1932), i.
    letter to Gilbert Elliot of Minto, 22 September 1764.
17 *Ibid*. i p436, p121; ii pp309-10; i p255.

[18]   Adam Smith, *The Wealth of Nations* (1776), v i-ii; Everyman's
       Library Edition (London 1971) ii p247, pp291-4.
[19]   Adam Ferguson, *An Essay on the History of Civil Society* (1776)
       ed. Duncan Forbes (Edinburgh 1966), p59.
[20]   John Gibson Lockhart, *Peter's Letters to his Kinsfolk* (Edinburgh
       1819), ii p359: letter lv.
[21]   Edwin Muir, *Scott and Scotland: the Predicament of the Scottish
       Writer* (London 1936), p137
[22]   John Gibson Lockhart, *Memoirs of Sir Walter Scott* (1837-8), ch. xv.
[23]   *The Letters of Sir Walter Scott*, ed. H J C Grierson (London 1932-7)
       ix p437: letter to James Ballantyne, 26-7 February 1826.
[24]   Sir Walter Scott, *The Letters of Malachi Malagrowther* (1826) *ed.* P
       H Scott (Edinburgh 1981). See also my *Walter Scott and Scotland*
       (Edinburgh 1981 and 1994) especially ch.7.
[25]   *Ibid*. p136.
[26]   Hugh MacDiarmid, *Lucky Poet: A Self-Study in Literature and
       Political Ideas* (London 1943), p203.
[27]   Alexander Murdoch, *The People Above: Politics and Administration
       in Mid-Eighteenth Century Scotland* (Edinburgh 1980), p106.
[28]   Sir Walter Scott, *The Letters of Malachi Malagrowther*, 9-10.
[29]   John Buchan, *Sir Walter Scott* (London 1932 and 1961), pp209-10.
[30]   Henry Cockburn, *Life of Francis Jeffrey* (Edinburgh 1872),
       pp151-153.
[31]   *Ibid*. p154.
[32]   Sir Walter Scott, *Journal* (Edinburgh 1891), p670: Entry for 24th
       March 1829.
[33]   John Gibson Lockhart, *Peter's Letters to his Kinsfolk* (Edinburgh
       1819), ii p356.
[34]   *Ibid*. ii p153.
[35]   *Ibid*. ii p4.
[36]   George Elder Davie, *The Democratic Intellect: Scotland and her
       Universities in the Nineteenth Century* (Edinburgh 1961), p337.
[37]   William Power, *My Scotland* (Edinburgh 1934), p296.
[38]   *The Letters of Sir Walter Scott*, ed. H J C Grierson (London 1932-7)
       ix p472: letter to J W Croker, 19 March 1826.
[39]   Edward Gibbon, *Autobiography* (London 1932: Everyman's
       Library) p81.

[40]   George Elder Davie, *op. cit.*, p.106 and p.58.

[41]   C P Snow in a speech in Edinburgh to the International Federation of Library Associations on 4 September 1961 (*The Scotsman*, 5 September 1961).

[42]   V H Galbraith in a speech to the Historical Association of Scotland on 1 March 1944 (*The Scotsman*, 2 March 1944)

[43]   James Grant, *Old and New Edinburgh* (London 1880), p110.

[44]   Henry Brougham in a speech in Edinburgh on 5 April 1825 (*The Scotsman*, 6 April 1825).

[45]   Elizabeth Hay, *Sambo Sahib* (Edinburgh 1981), p111.

[46]   Edwin Muir, *Scottish Journey* (1935), (Edinburgh 1979), pp3-4.

[47]   Henry Cockburn, *Journal* (Edinburgh 1874), ii pp31-2.

[48]   Edwin Muir, *Scott and Scotland: The Predicament of the Scottish Writer* (London 1936), p144.

[49]   Michael Hechter, *Internal Colonialism: The Celtic Fringe in British National Development* (London 1975), pp64, 73, 80-1.

[50]   R L Stevenson, "The Foreigner at Home" in *Memories and Portraits* (1887).

[51]   Michael Hechter, *op.cit.*, p117.

[52]   Sir Walter Scott, *The Letters of Malachi Malagrowther*, p143.

[53]   T S Eliot, *Notes Towards the Definition of Culture* (London 1948), p57.

[54]   Harold Orel, *The Scottish World: History and Cultures of Scotland* (London 1981), p12.

[55]   H W Thompson, *Henry Mackenzie: A Scottish Man of Feeling* (London and New York 1931), p1.

[56]   J K Galbraith in a BBC television programme in 1977.

[57]   Christopher Harvie, *Scotland and Nationalism: Scottish Society and Politics 1707-1977* (London 1977), p18.

[58]   J A Froude *quoted* by Professor Gordon Donaldson in his Inaugural Lecture in the University of Edinburgh, 1964.

[59]   Henry Thomas Buckle, *op. cit.*, p395.

[60]   Eric Linklater, *The Lion and the Unicorn* (London 1935), p130.

[61]   George Elder Davie, *op. cit.* pxvi.

[62]   J Watson in *Literature of the North*, *ed*. David Hewitt and Michael Spiller (Aberdeen 1983), p140.

[63]   Philip Mairet, *Pioneer of Sociology: The Life and Letters of Patrick Geddes* (London 1957), p68.

[64]   Tom Scott, *Introduction, The Penguin Book of Scottish Verse* (Harmondsworth 1970), p50.

[65]   Donald Dewar in *The Scottish Debate*, *ed*. Neil McCormick (Oxford 1970), p77.

[66]   Eric Linklater, *op.cit.*, pp26-7.

[67]   *Scottish Resources in Schools*, a discussion paper published by the Dundee College of Education for the Consultative Committee on the Curriculum, 1985.

[68]   James Campbell, *Invisible Country: a Journey Through Scotland* (London 1984), p83.

[69]   Andrew Dewar Gibb, *Scotland Resurgent* (Stirling 1950), p203.

THE UNION OF 1707

"A historical iniquity"
The Imposition of the Union

The Herald of 12 August 1995

No event in our history in the last 300 years has had more profound effects on Scotland than the Union of 1707, but there is deep misunderstanding of what it was and how it happened. For over 100 years Unionist propaganda has been trying hard to persuade us that it was an arrangement which Scotland wanted at the time for the sake of access to the English and colonial markets. Constant repetition has persuaded many people to believe this, but it is the opposite of the truth. The "incorporating" Union was forced on Scotland to serve English political and strategic purposes.

John Clerk of Penicuik was one of the members of the Scottish Parliament who voted for the Union. He afterwards wrote a book about it in Latin of which a translation has just been published by the Scottish History Society. He says that not even 1% of the Scottish people were in favour of the Union, but it was English policy "either to destroy us or force us into union". The Scots had to accept that "you cannot force your will on those stronger than yourself".

In defiance of the historical evidence, Unionists still try to push the same old line. Ian Lang wrote in a newspaper article a few months ago: "In 1707 Scotland sought and won full participation in the UK Parliament." Distortion could hardly go further. In a recent debate in Glasgow University, George Robertson made a slightly less extravagant claim that "the Union rests and has always rested on consent".

The theory that the Scots agreed to the Union for reasons of trade has also become part of accepted wisdom. It was evolved in the middle of the 19th

39

century by two historians, Macaulay and Burton, who wanted to find an explanation for the Scottish sacrifice of their independence. The modern English historian who has made an extensive study of the matter, P. W. J. Reilly, concluded that trade "hardly entered" into the real motives. In fact, from the Scottish point of view, considerations of trade weighed more heavily against the Union than for it. Andrew Fletcher of Saltoun and the merchant interest argued that the Treaty would be harmful to Scottish trade, that imports from England would destroy manufacturing industry in Scotland and that duties designed for English conditions would put impossible burdens on the Scottish economy. They were right. All the evidence is that the Scottish economy was seriously damaged by the Union. It took about 50 years to recover and then largely because of Scottish initiatives in new technologies in manufacturing and agriculture.

In any case such considerations had very little influence. The terms of the Union were dictated by the English Government and Scottish wishes and Scottish opinion were ignored. The Treaty was ratified by the Scottish Parliament after three months debate by a majority of 110 to 69, but the Parliament was not representative or subject to popular election. Contemporary sources on both sides of the question agree that the Union was massively unpopular.

Scotland at the start of the 18th century was weak and vulnerable, largely as a result of the Union of the Crowns in 1603. At that time and for the century which followed the monarch had actual, and not merely theoretical, power. This power was exercised through and on the advice of English ministers and in the interests of England. Scotland was still nominally independent but it had lost its international identity, control over foreign and trade policy and even the right to appoint the members of its own government. England's foreign wars damaged Scottish trade. Although Scotland contributed men and money, it was forgotten in the peace settlements and left virtually defenceless at home.

The Revolution of 1688-9 restored a degree of freedom to the Scottish Parliament. It could debate and decide as it pleased, but its Acts were still subject to royal assent and the officers of state (or, as we should now say, ministers) who sat in it, directed its debates and administered the government, were appointed and instructed by London.

Not content with these powers, the English government exercised other influences through patronage and bribery. The most remarkable coup of all was the recruitment of the Duke of Hamilton. He acted as the leader of the opposition in the Parliament of 1703 to 1707, and as such was cheered whenever he appeared in the streets of Edinburgh; but he repeatedly frustrated his own side. There is convincing evidence that he too was in the pay of the English government. Bribery was not only pervasive, but well targeted.

The disadvantages of this system of remote control were brought into sharp focus by the failure of the Darien scheme in 1700. As King of Scotland, William gave assent to the Scottish trading company. As King of England, he did his best to undermine it. English shareholders withdrew and English diplomatic pressure discouraged other European investment. In a great burst of patriotic fervour, the entire capital was subscribed in Scotland, amounting to about half of the money in circulation and the entire assets of many people. The venture collapsed, partly because it was ill-conceived and partly because of English hostility. To add to the misery, several years of bad summers and poor harvests caused actual starvation.

At the beginning of the 18th century there was general agreement in Scotland that indirect control from London was intolerable. An opportunity to escape from the joint monarchy, which was the source of the problem, arose in 1700 when the last of Queen Anne's children died. There was now no obvious or automatic successor to the throne. The English Parliament, without any consultation with Scotland, passed an Act of Succession in 1701, offering the throne to Sophia, Electress of Hanover, and her descendants. Not for the last time, they seem to have forgotten about Scotland, which was now free to make its own decision about the Succession.

This was the situation which faced the Scottish Parliament summoned in 1703. The instructions from London to the Commissioner, Queensberry, were to obtain acceptance of the Hanoverian Succession and the supply of money. This would have meant, of course, the preservation of indirect control. The Scottish Parliament had other ideas. Following Andrew Fletcher's analysis they passed the Act of Security, which provided either for the choice of a separate Successor or the transfer of all power from the throne to Parliament.

The English Government did not react until the Scottish Parliament showed its determination by passing the same Act again in 1704. England was confronted with what they saw as a threat to a vital national interest, the loss of control over Scotland. Early in 1705 the English Parliament passed an

Act calling for negotiation of a union with Scotland and the application of
sanctions if Scotland did not accept the same Succession by 25th December.

The Scottish Parliament were perfectly ready to discuss union, which up
to that time had generally meant any form of alliance or association and
which did not imply the loss of a separate Parliament. During the debate on
this Hamilton performed what he afterwards called his "signal service" to
the Court. One evening, after most of his supporters had left the House, he
suddenly proposed that the appointment of the Scottish Commissioners
should be left to the Queen. The Government seized this opportunity and it
was so decided. This meant in effect that both teams of negotiators were
appointed by the Queen's English ministers. Those on the Scottish side
were the Officers of State and some of their friends and protégés, with only
one exception, Lockhart of Carnwath. Under these circumstances genuine
negotiation was not to be expected.

There is no need to speculate about the nature of the discussions in London
in the summer of 1706 because we have information from the official minutes
and from accounts in the letters and memoirs of some of the participants.
Even before the formal talks started, Mar, the Secretary of State, wrote to
Carstares in Edinburgh: "They (the English) think all the notions about
foederal unions and forms a mere jest and chimera. I write this freely to
you, though it is not fit this should be known in Scotland, for fear of
discouraging people, and making them despair of the treaty. You see what
we are to treat of is not in our choice, and that we see the inconveniences of
treating an incorporating union only."

These inconveniences were exactly what followed. The Scots made a
token effort to preserve their separate Parliament, but the English would
not hear of it and the Scots gave way at once. That was the pattern
throughout. At intervals of a few days, meetings were held at which written
proposals were accepted with very little discussion. The Scottish Officers
of State were accustomed to acting on English instructions, as their letters
abundantly show. In this manner, the business was conducted with speed
and ease.

It was one thing to dictate terms in London; it was another to persuade
the Scottish Parliament to accept them. Much of the Treaty consists of
measures clearly designed to appeal to the self-interest of the classes
represented in Parliament: the guarantees of the Scottish legal system, the
heritable jurisdictions and the rights and privileges of the royal burghs.

These particular clauses were proposed by the Scots, but accepted with an alacrity which shows agreement in advance. Above all there was the ingenious Equivalent, a sum of £398,085, 10 shillings. It was said to be compensation to the Scots for accepting a share in the English National Debt, but also to the shareholders for the abolition of the Darien company. In any case it was to be repaid by the Scots through Excise Duty. "In fact," as Walter Scott wrote, "the Parliament of Scotland was bribed with the public money belonging to their own country. In this way, Scotland herself was made to pay the price given to her legislators for the sacrifice of her independence."

In addition there was an increase in straightforward bribery. When Lockhart was a member of the British Parliament in 1711 he was a member of a commission to enquire into public accounts. He discovered records of the secret disbursement of £20,000 through the Earl of Glasgow in 1706. Two letters have survived in which Glasgow confirms this and says that if it had become known at the time, "the Union had certainly broken".

Behind all this was the ultimate persuader, discreet but real military intimidation. In 1703 the English Lord Treasurer, Godolphin, made an unmistakable threat in a letter to the Scottish Chancellor, Seafield, in which he reminded him of the great increase in the wealth and power of England. During the debate on the Treaty in the Scottish Parliament in 1706, English troops were moved to the Border.

The English Government thus achieved the Union of 1707 by means of a remarkably sophisticated and elaborate operation. It involved spying, infiltration and propaganda (in which the skilful and tireless Daniel Defoe was engaged); the threat of economic sanctions and of military force; systematic bribery and seductive appeals to the self-interest of the few men who had to be won over. It may seem like an excessive effort to win a few votes in the Scottish Parliament, but great issues were at stake.

The English aim was the final achievement of a centuries-old objective, to bring Scotland under their control and remove a potential threat to their northern border.

To Scotland it meant the loss of the independence defended against heavy odds for more than 300 years. The law, the church, the burghs and education continued as before; but they were all subject to interference by the new Parliament of Great Britain. In this Scotland, with about the same representation as Cornwall, was in an impotent minority. According to the

Treaty, the Parliaments of both England and Scotland were abolished and
replaced by this new creation. In practice, only the Parliament of Scotland
disappeared, but that of England continued with the addition of the few
Scottish members. In the words of Tom Scott, it was "a historical iniquity
with no right but might behind it".

An Eye-Witness Account
Lockhart of Carnwath's 'Memoirs'

The Scotsman, 1 December 1995

On 7th December an edition of Lockhart of Carnwath's *Memoirs** will be published for the first time since 1817. This is a real bombshell of a book. It is a frank exposure of the events which led to the Union of 1707 by a man who was directly involved. Lockhart was a member of the Scottish Parliament from 1703 to 1707 and he was one of the Commissioners who went to London in 1706 to negotiate, or more accurately receive, the terms of the Treaty. The *Memoirs* have long been recognised by historians as one of the principal sources for the period. Lockhart is fiercely partisan and he makes no secret of his feelings. On the other hand, his account of events is consistent with all the other evidence and he has never been proved wrong on any point of substance. It is also a very lively historical narrative, full of tension, suspense and drama, and ultimately tragic in its conclusion. Lockhart's sentences are sometimes Latinate and involved, but he is also a master of the pungent phrase. His *Memoirs* are the best thing of this kind in our literature since *John Knox's History of the Reformation.*

Why then has there been no new edition since 1817? This is indeed very curious and significant. The historian, Hume Brown, speculated in his Ford Lectures in Oxford in 1914 about the reasons for the general ignorance among Scots of the events leading to the Union, "one of the most fateful periods in their national history". The first reason, he thought, was a sense of shame, "an unconscious instinct" which made us try to forget. The Union was a subject which the Scots "must regard with mingled feelings, among which pride is not predominant... A people does not gladly turn its eyes to a period when its representative men, whether from their own natural failings or as a result of temporary circumstances, compromise the national character in the eyes of the world". Hume Brown may well be right that the subject was simply too painful to contemplate, but he goes on to suggest an additional reason. This is that the general ignorance of the circumstances of the Union might be due to the absence of a contemporary account which could "permanently stamp its characters and its events on the mind of posterity".

Lockhart's *Memoirs* is precisely such an account. The trouble from the point of view of those, like Hume Brown, who wanted to attempt to justify the Union (and that was the predominant attitude in the 19th century) was that Lockhart gave the game away in an unflinching exposure of a very sordid transaction. If you wanted to conceal the facts and maintain that the Union was an act of enlightened statesmanship, then you certainly did not want to encourage people to read Lockhart. His book has been suppressed by censorship through consensus. For this reason, it has never received the recognition which it deserves as a work of literature as well as an important historical source.

Sir Walter Scott was aware of the *Memoirs* . He wrote to Robert Cadell in May 1829: "I wish you could get me the Lockhart papers (use of them) two volumes quarto. I have not brought them from the country and they are indispensable to copy of tales". The reference is to his *Tales of a Grandfather*, which Scott was writing at the time. Thanks largely to Lockhart, Scott's account of the Union in that book is the most honest and revealing of any written in the 19th century. He draws heavily on Lockhart and quotes, for example, the evidence of bribery which Lockhart had uncovered. Byron, too, knew about the *Memoirs*. In 1822 he was looking for an oppressed country to liberate, for he considered others before he decided on Greece. He wrote from Pisa on 16th May 1822 to John Murray in London: "Could you send me the Lockhart papers a publication on Scotch affairs of sometime since". We do not know if the two volumes ever reached him. If they had, they might have turned his crusading zeal towards his native country. The *Memoirs* had the capacity, I think, to have that effect.

After the Union, Lockhart became the member for Midlothian in the new British Parliament. He was active in trying to mitigate some of the consequences of the Union in such matters as a malt tax which treated Scotland unfairly and violated the Treaty. He was a prime mover in the attempt which followed to dissolve the Treaty. As a member of a Parliamentary Commission appointed in 1711 to examine public accounts he was able to uncover evidence of secret payments to members of the Scottish Parliament in 1706 during the debate on the Treaty. He added a report about this in an Appendix to the *Memoirs* as a "further discovery" which had come to light since they were written. Lockhart did not mince words about people of whom he disapproved. He admitted as much himself in his first *Preface*, "my indignation against the betrayers of my country is so great, I never could, nor will, speak or write otherwise of them". (Although, even in these cases, he often admits their good points.) Facts about the sequence and nature of events are another matter and here Lockhart stands up very well to close examination. No one, as far as I am aware, has ever detected him in any serious inaccuracy or misrepresentation. I have been through the evidence as carefully and minutely as I could in the course of writing two books on the period. I have often been struck by the way in which Lockhart's account is consistent with the rest of the evidence. Very often his account is supported by documents of which he could not have been aware and which have come to light very many years later.

The most obvious example of this is over the issue of bribery. Lockhart's own account in the appendix to the *Memoirs*, is convincing enough, with the production of the original documents to a Parliamentary Commission. Long afterwards other documents have been discovered which confirm his account beyond any possibility of doubt. Time and again, when Lockhart's version of events is compared with the private correspondence of men on the Government side, it is impossible not to be struck by his reliability as a witness and by his knowledge and understanding of the motives and attitudes of his political opponents. There is, for example, ample confirmation from a host of witnesses, Mar, Seafield, Clerk, Defoe and many others, about the hostility of the people of Scotland to the Treaty and the reaction of the crowds on the streets of Edinburgh.

The publication of this new edition restores at long last an important book to the canon of Scottish history and literature.

* *Scotland's Ruine: Lockhart of Carnwath's Memoirs of the Union*, edited by Daniel Szechi with an Introduction by Paul H. Scott (Association for Scottish Literary Studies).

Sir John Clerk of Penicuik,
a Reluctant Unionist

Scottish Literary Journal, Winter 1995; Supplement no. 43

Sir John Clerk of Penicuik (1676-1755) was a man of great diversity of talents and interests, antiquary, composer, architect, poet and patron of architects and poets. "All in all," Ian Gordon Brown has said, "he was the most notable virtuoso in the Scotland of his day."[1] He was also a politician who was closely involved with economic and financial questions. As a member of the Scottish Parliament from 1703 to 1707 he played a part in bringing about the Union. As a reward, he was made a Baron of the Scottish Court of Exchequer, a grant which kept him in affluent ease for the rest of his life.

Clerk was at first a reluctant unionist. He tells us in his *Memoirs* that when he was invited to become one of the Scottish Commissioners for the Treaty, he was about to refuse, "for I had observed a great backwardness in the Parliament of Scotland for an union with England of any kind whatsoever".[2] Queensberry, the High Commissioner (who was a cousin of Clerk's first wife) "threatened to withdraw all friendship" and therefore all hope of patronage. Clerk accepted and from then onwards he supported the Unionist cause.

Douglas Duncan has now given us, as the annual volume of the Scottish History Society, a translation from the Latin of part of an extraordinary attempt at self-justification, a history, *De Imperio Britannico*, of which the full text of about 360,000 words occupied Clerk for forty years. Clerk tells us that he spent eighteen years reading Latin histories as a conscious preparation for the task. His decision to write was reinforced by the publication in 1714 of the pirated edition of George Lockhart of Carnwath's *Memoirs*.[3] Clerk apparently wanted not only to reply to Lockhart's exposure of the Union, but to outshine him by adopting the *gravitas* of Latin and by extending his historical range by going back to the time of the Romans. He wanted to represent the course of Scottish history as a process leading to Union.

This History was not Clerk's only attempt to justify himself. In 1730 he wrote a short pamphlet, *Observations on the present circumstances of Scotland*, which was published by the Scottish History Society in 1965 in their Volume X Miscellany. In 1744 he wrote a *Testamentary Memorial concerning the Union of the Two Kingdoms of Scotland and England in 1707* for his "Children, Brothers and Friends". It is included as one of the appendices in the present volume. Why did Clerk protest so much? Duncan in his excellent Introduction says: "The sincerity of his life-long defences of union can hardly be doubted, but behind them lay an uncomfortable, unacknowledged sense of the need for self-justification."[4] It was not entirely "unacknowledged' because in his *Memorandum* about the *History* (which is also included in this volume) Clerk admits that one of his motives was to vindicate his own conduct.[5] There are many signs of tension and disquiet in the three works.

The first point is Clerk's evident admiration for Andrew Fletcher of Saltoun, the leading opponent of the Union. In his *Memoirs* Clerk described Fletcher as "a very Honest Man, and meant well in everything he said and did, except in cases where his humoure, passion and prejudices were suffered to get the better of his reasone".[6] In the three works now under discussion Clerk quotes Fletcher frequently and always refers to him with respect. In the *History* he calls him "a most learned and eloquent man"[7], in the *Observation* "an eminent gentleman"[8] and in the *Testamentary Memorial*, "a very learned gentleman".[9]

Clerk also emphatically agrees with Fletcher's analysis of the situation in which Scotland found itself as a consequence of the Union of the Crowns: nominal independence, but actual control and exploitation by England. He makes the point repeatedly in all three of the works, and, if anything, his language grows stronger with the years. In the *Observation* he says that the Scottish Parliament, Privy Council, Treasury and Exchequer after 1603 were all "subservient to such administrators as the chief ministers in England thought fit to recommend to the Soveraign ...We were in a state of absolute bondage to England".[10] In the *History*: "Scotland's trade ... was sacrificed to English greed" and "Scotland was left with nothing but its name and ruled like a province of England".[11] In the *Testamentary Memorial* his language is at least as strong as any used by Fletcher. He says that after 1603 Scotland "came from time to time under the Government of such necessitous rapacious & mercenary Court-favourites as the Ministers of State in England thought fit to appoint".[12] Clerk followed Fletcher also in his account of the disadvantages suffered by Scotland because of her involuntary involvement in England's wars after 1603, as in this passage from the *History*:

> Trade declined daily as a result of the war against France, which the Scots, with nothing to gain from it, were called upon by England to join. Their merchant ships were seized by the enemy and pillaged, their young men pressed into the army overseas to the detriment of industry. All of which could have been borne if the Scots had been allowed some credit or advantage when peace came, but, on the contrary, they were treated by the English and confederate leaders not as allies but mercenaries. The treaty of Ryswick ignored Scotland, did not even mention it, made no attempt even indirectly to offer reparation for its losses. But Scotland had come to expect such rewards for serving the English cause.[13]

When the Scottish Commissioners, including Clerk, went to London in 1706 for the negotiations (if that is the right word), their treatment was equally discouraging. The Scottish Secretary of State, the Earl of Mar, wrote in a letter at the time: "What we are to treat of is not in our choice."[14] Clerk's own account is fully consistent with this. The business was normally conducted by the exchange of written drafts which were usually accepted with little, if any, discussion. The Scots rebelled, however, when it came to the proposal that the English representation in the two Houses of Parliament should be unchanged, but the Scots reduced to 16 Peers in the Lords and 38 Members in the Commons. Clerk says that the Scots reacted "with the utmost dismay and indignation".[15] For once the English agreed to a joint discussion which Clerk duly reports. The Scots proposed that either the new British Parliament should have a proportional allocation of seats between the two countries or that the two existing Parliaments should be combined. The English argued that considerations of justice or equality could not be applied to their system and that to alter it would put their whole society at risk. "Union would be obstructed if the ancient constitution of the parliament of England were to be changed in any way."[16] Of course a very drastic change in the ancient constitution of Scotland was under discussion, but, as Clerk reports a unionist speaker at a later stage: "You cannot force your will on those stronger than yourself."[17] The English eventually agreed to increase Scottish representation in the Commons to 45 (about the same as

Cornwall). The Scottish representative Peers remained at 16 (although the English bishops alone in the Lords numbered 26).

Clerk is invariably frank about the rejection of the Union by the great majority of the Scottish people. In *Observations* he says that "the Articles [of the Treaty] were confirmed in the Parliament of Scotland contrary to the inclinations of at least three-fourths of the Kingdom".[18] In the *History* he goes even further: "Not even one per cent" of the people approved; but he thought that Parliament was "wiser than the people".[19]

This was the same Parliament which the same members (apart from the replacement of a few who had died) which in 1703 and 1704 had approved the Act of Security by a large majority. This Act, which substantially adopted the ideas of Andrew Fletcher, was an emphatic assertion of Scottish independence. It called on the death of Queen Anne either for a return to a separate Scottish monarchy or for the transfer of all power from the Monarch to Parliament. Clerk hardly addresses the question of how it came about that a majority of this same Parliament only two years later in a sustained debate over three and a half months consistently voted with the Government and for its own absorption as an insignificant minority in the Parliament of England. The Government had achieved a position where it counted on a majority even against proposals which were unquestionably in the interest of Scotland. As Clerk records them, they included a suggestion that the joint Parliament would meet in Scotland at least one year in three; exemption of Scots from press gangs for seven years; reduction of Scottish land tax; exemption from malt tax and of Scots from the English Test Act.[20] On all of them a majority voted as the Government's "led horses", as Lockhart of Carnwath described them.[21]

How did the Government achieve control of these "led horses"? Clerk touches lightly on this delicate subject; "I am aware that the successful passage of Union has been attributed by some to the bounty of the royal purse, but that report (as I shall later show) was based more on guesswork than on facts that ever came to light".[22] In fact, Lockhart exposed hard evidence of bribery and much more has since emerged;[23] but straightforward bribery was the least of it. The Treaty itself contained provisions ingeniously designed to appeal to the self-interest of precisely the classes represented in Parliament: the preservation of heritable jurisdictions, of the rights of the burghs and of the Scottish legal system and, above all, the arrangement of the Equivalent to compensate the shareholders of the Darien Company.

There was also the distribution of titles and lucrative offices and Clerk himself was a recipient of one of them.

This does not necessarily mean that Clerk cynically and deliberately supported the Union, after his initial hesitation, only because he was aiming at the sort of reward which he eventually acquired. I agree with the point made by Douglas Duncan in his Introduction, which I have already quoted, that it is difficult to doubt Clerk's sincerity, to a degree at least. He had, I think, persuaded himself or tried hard to believe, that the Union was preferable to its probable alternative.

He is quite specific in all three of the documents about what he saw as the alternative: military conquest and the imposition of worse terms. In the *Observation* he says that "it was absolutely against the interest of England to suffer Scotland to grow rich in a separate state". An example was their reaction to the Darien scheme where "the English were so far from assisting us that they did all in their power to ruine us". If Scotland opted for independence and a separate monarchy, "in the end the whole country would fall under the Domination of England by right of conquest".[24] In the *History* he refers again to the control exercised by England: "But as soon as they perceived that we had seen through their trick, roused ourselves from sleep and aspired to better things [an evident allusion to the Act of Security] it became their necessary policy either to destroy us or to force us into union on well-defined terms".[25] As in other cases, he is still more outspoken in his last word in his *Testamentary Memorial*: "England as being at least four times more numerous in people than Scotland wou'd have found little difficulty in subdueing us ... and in treating us ignominiously & cruelly as a conquered province."[26]

As I have said, Clerk had a special interest in economic and financial matters and it was with those that he was concerned in the Court of Exchequer. He discussed the economy and foreign trade of Scotland in the three works, but nowhere suggests that considerations of that kind were of particular importance in the question of the Union. As Christopher Smout says in his Introduction to the *Observation*, Clerk's conclusion in 1730 was that economically since the Union: "things have not really got worse but have remained on balance very much the same".[27] Clerk says that what Scotland needs is "an assiduous attention to virtue and industry", but he does not suggest that the Union by itself was calculated to bring economic benefits. There is one reference to economic factors having a "great influence with many": but with his expert knowledge of the facts, this is evidently not a view which he shares.[28] For both Scotland and England he regards matters of state security as decisive, for Scotland the need to avoid invasion and conquest by England and for England the need to secure her northern border against the risk of an independent Scotland again acting in alliance with France. In his *Testamentary Memorial* Clerk describes the great celebration and rejoicing in London on 1st May 1707 when the Union came into force: "The joy was universal & indeed the English nation had never better reasone having been delivered from the terrible fears and Apprehensions they were under from Scotland."[29] There was no such celebration in Edinburgh.

Clerk therefore had accepted a lucrative and life-long office as a reward for supporting a policy of surrender rather than risk the possibility of attack by a more powerful neighbour which he regarded as greedy and ill-disposed. Such a policy may be prudent, but it is hardly glorious. I think that it is very likely that Clerk had suppressed feelings of guilt and disquiet. He had accompanied Fletcher intellectually so far that he might well have misgivings about not following him to the logical conclusion. At the end of his *Memorandums concerning this History* he said that he might have had it printed in his own lifetime if it had not been for the fact that it would provoke criticism and he was "now too old for disputes of this kind".[30] He evidently felt vulnerable.

And indeed, why did Clerk impose on himself the heavy and unnatural task of writing a history in Latin which had long ceased to be the language of serious works on such a subject? Since he made no attempt to have it published who was he trying to persuade except himself? It looks to me very much like an act of penance and contrition to assuage a sense of guilt.

Douglas Duncan says that "Clerk's skills as a historian were limited" and that even in the part dealing with events in which he was a participant he "tells us little that we do not know already and steadfastly overlooks much that we do ... We are left with a major curiosity".[31] All of this is true. Clerk's account of the debates in the Scottish Parliament might have been a valuable source, but he groups points from the speeches together without distinguishing the speakers. We do not know the extent to which they are an accurate record or a rhetorical construction by Clerk himself.

In spite of all of this, I think that Clerk's *History*, taken together with his other works, does throw a useful light on these momentous events. Douglas Duncan (whose translation is as fluent as his Introduction is lucid) has done a valuable service in making it available. It is, after all, the only sustained attempt by a participant on the government side to explain and justify his position. As Duncan says, it tells us little that is new. On the other hand, it confirms much that we knew or had good reason to believe (as I have argued elsewhere):[32] that the Union was massively unpopular in Scotland, on whom it was imposed for English reasons of state, and that considerations of trade played very little part.

References

Abbreviations
SHS (1892) *Memoirs of Sir John Clerk of Penicuik, ed.* John M Gray (Scottish History Society 1892)
SHS (1965) Scottish History Society vol. x: Miscellany (1965)
SHS (1993) Sir John Clerk of Penicuik, *History of the Union of Scotland and England, ed.* Douglas Duncan (Scottish History Society 1993)

1   Ian Gordon Brown, The Clerks of Penicuik (Penicuik House Preservation Trust 1987), p13.
2   SHS (1892), p58.
3   By a fortunate coincidence, an edition of George Lockhart of Carnwath's *Memoirs* has just been published as the annual volume of the ASLS for 1995.
4   SHS (1993), p7.
5   *Ibid*. p175.
6   SHS (1892), pp48-9.
7   SHS (1993), p112.
8   SHS (1965), p185.
9   SHS (1993), p187.
10   SHS (1965), pp184,192.
11   SHS (1993), pp79,81.
12   *Ibid*. p184.
13   *Ibid*. p82.
14   *State Papers and Letters Addressed to William Carstares, ed.* Joseph McCormick (Edinburgh 1774), pp743-4.
15   SHS (1993), p85, fn.2.

16   *Ibid*. p87.
17   *Ibid*. p162.
18   SHS (1965), p192.
19   SHS (1993), pp118,173.
20   *Ibid*. pp133,138,147,148,155.
21   George Lockhart of Carnwath, *The Lockhart Papers* (London 1817) i p162.
22   SHS (1965), p191.
23   Paul H Scott, 1707: *The Union of Scotland and England* (Edinburgh 1979 and 1994), pp39-44, and *Andrew Fletcher and the Treaty of Union* (Edinburgh 1992 and 1994), pp83, 119-20, 182-4 and passim.
24   SHS (1965), p191.
25   SHS (1993), pp172-3.
26   *Ibid*. p186.
27   SHS (1965), p182.
28   *Ibid*. pp192,212.
29   SHS (1993), p202.
30   *Ibid*. p178.
31   *Ibid*. p1.
32   In particular the books mentioned in fn. 23 above.

BURNS AND SCOTT

WHO HELPED US TO SURVIVE, IN SPITE OF IT

Robert Burns, Patriot

Paper for the International Bicentenary Burns Conference,
11-13 January 1996, at Strathclyde University.

It is difficult to speak about patriotism in this cynical age. We all instinctively remember that Samuel Johnson said that it was the last refuge of a scoundrel. Boswell's explanation when he recorded this is less familiar. Johnson, he says, "did not mean a real and generous love of our country, but that pretended patriotism which so many, in all ages and countries, have made a cloak for self-interest".[1] A "real and generous", and I should add passionate, love for Scotland is a good description of a feeling and conviction which Burns clearly and repeatedly revealed in his writing, both in verse and prose.

Burns himself tells us how he thought it began. In his famous autobiographical letter to Dr. John Moore on 2nd August 1787 he said: "the story of Wallace poured a Scottish prejudice in my veins which will boil along there till the flood-gates of life shut in eternal rest." Thomas Carlyle said that Burns was too modest when he called his "deep and generous" patriotism a prejudice. And he added:

> We hope, there is a patriotism founded on something better than prejudice; that our country may be dear to us, without injury to our philosophy; that in loving and justly prizing all other lands, we may prize justly, and yet love before all others, our own stern Motherland ... Certainly in no heart did the love of country ever burn with warmer glow than in that of Burns.[2]

Carlyle was right. In this sense, Burns was a patriot, or, if you prefer, a nationalist, especially because he deeply resented Scotland's loss of independence.

Consistently with this, Burns revered Wallace as our great national hero.
One of the reasons why he corresponded so eagerly with Mrs. Dunlop was
that she claimed descent from Wallace's family. In his first letter to her on
15 November 1786 he referred to Wallace as her "illustrious Ancestor, the
SAVIOUR OF HIS COUNTRY". He said that he had walked to the Leglen
wood, which was associated with Wallace, "with as much devout enthusiasm
as ever Pilgrim did to Loretto" and that his "heart glowed with a wish to
make a song equal to his merits". He used similar language many times in
his letters and poems, as in the "Epistle to William Simpson":

> At Wallace name, What Scottish blood
> But boils up in a spring-tide flood?
> Oft have our fearless fathers strode
> By Wallace' side,
> Still pressing onward, red-wat-shod,
> Or glorious dy'd.

If Burns placed Wallace first, no doubt because of his humbler origin,
uncompromising patriotism and dreadful end, he also held Bruce in high
regard. He refers to both of them in a letter to Robert Muir on 26 August
1787, where he describes the first day of his tour to the Highlands:

> This morning I knelt at the tomb of Sir John the Graham, the gallant
> friend of the immortal Wallace; and two hours ago I said a fervent prayer
> for Old Caledonia over the hole in a blue whinstone, where Robert de
> Bruce fixed his royal standard on the banks of Bannockburn.

Burns's diaries of his Border and Highland tours consist mostly of very
brief notes, but his entry about this event is passionate. He imagines his
"heroic countrymen" approaching "the oppressive, insulting, blood-thirsty
foe", and "gloriously triumphant, exulting in their heroic royal leader and
rescued liberty and independence".

These thoughts on the field of Bannockburn immediately suggest the
words of "Scots Wha Hae", although the song was not written until sixteen
years later on about 30 August 1793. He describes the circumstances in a
letter to George Thomson, where he refers to the old air, "Hey Tuttie Taitie"
and then says:

There is a tradition, which I have met with in many places of Scotland, that it was Robert Bruce's March at the battle of Bannockburn.—This thought in my yesternight's evening walk, warmed me to a pitch of enthusiasm on the theme of Liberty and Independence, which I threw into a kind of Scots Ode, fitted to the air, that one might suppose to be the gallant ROYAL SCOT'S address to his heroic followers on that eventful morning.

At the end of the song he wrote: "So may God ever defend the cause of Truth and Liberty, as he did that day! Amen!" There is a further postscript to the letter: "the accidental recollection of that glorious struggle for Freedom, associated with the glowing ideas of some other struggles of the same nature, *not quite so ancient*, roused my rhyming mania."

What were these other struggles? Burns may have been thinking generally of French revolutionary ideas, but there was another event much nearer home and of a precise coincidence of date. On the same 30 August the trial of Thomas Muir of Huntershill for sedition began in Edinburgh. Muir, who advocated parliamentary reform and Scottish independence, was sentenced to transportation. In "Scots Wha Hae", therefore, Burns was drawing a parallel between Bruce's struggle for the independence of Scotland and the situation in his own time. Murray Pittock has pointed out that the song also uses Jacobite language. "For Scotland's King and Law" is a Jacobite phrase, and "chains and slaverie" could refer to the Jacobite prisoners who had been transported as slaves to the colonies. Pittock says that "the idea of a heroic, traditional Scotland as having to wage perpetual war against English might and gold in order to secure its very existence was one central to Jacobite images of native heroism".[3]

Burns himself said in a letter of 15 December 1793 to Mrs Dunlop that he was "really proud" of "Scots Wha Hae". Carlyle, in the essay which I have already quoted, said of it that so long as we have warm blood, "it will move in fierce thrills under this war-ode; the best ... ever written by any pen". Tom Crawford described it as "the noblest of all Burns's national songs" and David Murison as "a kind of national anthem of a nation that may even yet find the moral courage to sing it".[4] It may seem paradoxical that a man of egalitarian spirit like Burns should have looked back nostalgically, not only to Bruce, but the entire line of the Scottish monarchy. In his "Address to Edinburgh", for instance:

> Edina! Scotia's darling seat!
> All hail thy palaces and tow'rs,
> Where once, beneath a Monarch's feet
> Sat legislation's sov'reign pow'rs.

That last line is quite specific. His regret for the loss of the Scottish monarchy is regret for the loss of sovereignty and legislative power. His bitter sense of loss and his Jacobitism are even more apparent in the lines "written on the Window of an Inn in Stirling":

> Here Stewarts once in glory reign'd,
> And laws for Scotland's weal ordain'd;
> The injured Stewart line is gone,
> A race outlandish fills their throne:
> An idiot race, to honour lost —
> Who knows them best despise them most.

This did not mean that Burns wanted to see a return to arbitrary monarchy. He had a sophisticated sense of historical change. A letter which he sent to the editor of the *Edinburgh Evening Courant* on 8 November 1788 was no doubt written, as David Daiches has said, "to put himself right with officialdom" and "free himself to engage with Jacobite song";[5] but it also insisted that past events should not be judged by contemporary standards and that allowances must be made for the circumstances of the time.

Burns had particularly strong feelings about Mary, Queen of Scots, whom he called, in a letter of 25 April 1791 to Lady Winifred Constable "our greatly injured, lovely Scottish Queen". The English Elizabeth, on the other hand, in a letter of 28 February 1791 to John Moore, was "the infernal Bess Tudor". Burns's "Lament of Mary Queen of Scots" is deeply compassionate.

These feelings for the "injured Stewart line", more, I think because they were Scottish than because they were royal, were no doubt an element in Burns's Jacobitism; but there were others which were probably even more compelling. George Rosie has recently drawn attention to a passage in the writings of Hugh Miller where he suggests that Burns was in a state of intellectual confusion in professing both Jacobitism and Jacobinism at the same time.[6] In fact, this combination of ideas was not unusual and was certainly not confined to Burns. There were solid reasons for it. Jacobitism in Scotland was largely a patriotic, nationalist attempt to overthrow the Union. Also, as Murray Pittock has argued, Jacobite and Jacobin shared the view that the Hanoverians had created "something rotten in the state of Scotland" and that there was a need to defend traditional values against an oppressor for whom money was all that mattered.[7]

In supporting Jacobitism, Burns knew exactly what he was doing. He did not imagine that a Stewart could be restored to the throne. It was an expression of his detestation of the Union and of the arrogance and corruption of wealth. Walter Scott, who had Jacobite leanings himself, wrote of Burns that "a youth of his warm imagination and ardent patriotism", brought up at that time could "hardly escape Jacobitism".[8] Burns wrote or adapted about thirty Jacobite songs and they include some of his best and most passionate.

Andrew Noble has suggested that Burns's analysis of the Scottish situation is as valid now as it was in his time. In Noble's words, Burns was concerned with "the corrupting politics and psychology generated by the Union; the degeneration of parliament and other British civic and fiscal institutions, causing increasing disparity between rich and poor".[9] All of these things are at least as obvious now as they were in the eighteenth century.

There are other ways in which the ideas of Burns are still apposite to our present situation. He wrote in a letter to Mrs Dunlop on 10 April 1790: "Alas! have I often said to myself, what are all the boasted advantages which my country reaps from the Union, that can counterbalance the annihilation of her Independence, and even her very name!" That is precisely how many of us still feel. The same is true of

> We're bought and sold for English gold,
> Such a parcel of rogues in a nation!

The theme and refrain, Kinsley tells us, were current before Burns made them into a powerful and passionate statement. We find James Boswell, for example, making virtually the same point many years earlier. When he came across a copy of the text of the Declaration of Arbroath in Leipzig in October 1760, he wrote in his Journal:

> I felt true patriot sorrow. O infamous rascals, who sold the honour of your country to a nation against which our ancestors supported themselves with so much glory ... Alas, poor Scotland.

In the 19th century historians, with the honourable exception of Walter
Scott, did their best to play down the role of bribery in securing a majority
for the Union in the Scottish parliament. Modern scholarship has proved
beyond doubt that Boswell and Burns were right.

Burns's nationalism derived from a deep love of Scotland which he
repeatedly expressed. To the Earl of Eglinton on 11 January 1787, for
instance: "There is scarcely anything to which I am so feelingly alive as
the honour and welfare of old Scotia." To Mrs Dunlop on 22 March 1787:
"The appellation of a Scotch Bard is by far my highest pride; to continue to
deserve it is my most exalted ambition. — Scottish scenes, and Scottish
story are the themes I could wish to sing". And in the "Epistle to the
Gudewife of Wauchope House":

> E'en then, a wish (I mind its pow'r),
> A wish that to my latest hour
>   Shall strongly heave my breast,
> That I for poor auld Scotland's sake
> Some usefu plan or book could make
>   Or sing a sang at least

That last statement was not a rhetorical flourish, but a serious declaration of
intent. He approached his self-imposed task of collecting, making or
amending Scots songs in precisely this spirit. Although pitifully short of
money, he refused to take any payment for the work. He wrote to George
Thomson, the publisher of the *Select Collection of Scottish Airs* on 16
September 1792:

> As to any remuneration, you may think my songs either above or below
> price; for they shall absolutely be one or the other. — In the honest
> enthusiasm with which I embark in your undertaking, to talk of money,
> wages, fee, hire & etc would be downright sodomy of soul.

He attributed the same patriotic motive to others. When he wrote to Sir
John Sinclair in August 1791 about his *Statistical Account*, he called it
"your patriotic publication". He used the same phrase in a letter to James
Johnson on 19 June 1789 about his *Scots Musical Museum*.

In his autobiographical letter to John Moore, Burns said that it was after coming across Fergussons's Scotch Poems that he "strung my wildly-sounding, rustic lyre with emulating vigour". Both in verse and prose he paid many tributes to Ramsay and Fergusson as his models and inspiration, from the reference to them both in the Preface to the Kilmarnock edition to the inscription which he placed on Fergusson's grave: "My elder brother in misfortune / By far my elder brother in the muse." Like Burns, Ramsay and Fergusson wrote in Scots, and like him again, both were strongly nationalist in feeling and wrote poems against the Union. Does this suggest that writing poetry in Scots was in itself a nationalist act of defiance against the prevailing pressures of Anglicisation?

No doubt Burns wrote in Scots at least partly because it pleased him and came naturally. He wrote to George Thomson on 10 October 1774: "These English songs gravel me to death. — I have not that command of the language that I have of my native tongue. — In fact, I think my ideas are more barren in English than in Scottish." No one can doubt that he was right. On the other hand, he was under pressure from the literary grandees of the time to write in English. Burns often said that Henry Mackenzie was one of his favourite authors and that his *Man of Feeling* was a book which he prized next to the Bible. The same Mackenzie wrote the first review of the Kilmarnock Edition and in it he regretted that Burns wrote in a "provincial dialect" which was read with difficulty even in Scotland and in England "cannot be read at all".[10] Pressure like this could only be resisted by strong conviction.

Burns told George Thomson on 16 September 1792 that he had an "enthusiastic attachment to the poetry and Music of old Caledonia". This was an enthusiasm which he often expressed in his letters and Commonplace Book. He was determined to preserve the melodies of Scottish songs by writing new words where the old ones had been lost, were inadequate or where only the refrain survived. It was a patriotic labour of love similar in spirit to Walter Scott's collection of the Border Ballads. Burns began to contribute songs to Johnson's *Scots Musical Museum* in November 1787 and to Thomson's *Select Collection of Scottish Airs* in September 1792. He contributed 213 songs to Johnson and 114 to Thomson. With the important exception of "Tam o' Shanter", this meant that for the last nine years of his life Burns's writing of poetry was almost entirely devoted to songs.

There are those, and they include R. L. Stevenson, who regret this concentration on song and regard it as a degeneration of his powers. In his

essay on Burns, Stevenson wrote: "The man who had written a volume of
masterpieces in six months, during the remainder of his life rarely found
courage for any more sustained effort than a song." He went on to speak of
a "loss of moral courage" and said that it was melancholy that "a hand that
seemed capable of moving mountains, should have spent his later years in
whittling cherry-stones". Cedric Thorpe Davie was right, I think, to protest
about this attitude.[11] Scottish song is one of our greatest national treasures
and it would be immeasurably poorer without Burns's formidable
contribution.

Alexander Scott has suggested that there were two reasons for the decline
in Burns's satirical writing after the publication of the Kilmarnock edition
in 1786:"rootlessness and respectability". Burns was rootless because he
had left the community which had given him the substance for his attacks
on religious orthodoxy and aristocratic privilege, and respectable because
he had become an officer in the Excise.[12] That last point is probably the
main reason, and in fact the dates nearly coincide. Burns began to collaborate
seriously with the *Scots Musical Museum* in November 1787 and in January
1788 he wrote to Robert Graham of Fintry to solicit his patronage for an
appointment in the Excise. He began work as an Excise Officer in September
1789, and was therefore a civil servant of a government that was in a state
of panic fear of revolutionary ideas from France. Muir and the others who
were sentenced to transportation in 1793 were no more revolutionary in
their ideas than Burns himself and he had even attempted to send guns to
France to support the Revolution.

Burns clearly understood his vulnerability. He wrote to Mrs Dunlop on 6
December 1792 about an episode in the theatre in Dumfries when "God
save the King" had been hissed and the French revolutionary song, "Ça ira"
repeatedly called for:

> For me, I am a *Placeman*, you know, a very humble one indeed, Heaven
> knows, but still so much so as to gag me from joining in the cry. — What
> my private sentiments are, you will find out without an interpreter.

His caution was not sufficient to prevent a denunciation of him as a person
disaffected to Government, and the Board of Excise ordered an enquiry.
He sent two abject and frantic letters to his patron, Robert Graham. Even
dismissal from the service, without any more serious penalty, would, he

wrote on 31 December 1792, turn his wife and family adrift "without the necessary support of a miserable existence". In the second letter of 5 January 1793 he went through the humiliation of obligatory conformity; "As to Reform Principles, I look upon the British Constitution, as settled at the Revolution, to be the most glorious Constitution on earth, or that perhaps the wit of man can frame". (The Revolution in this case is, of course, that of 1688-89, when Scotland was still nominally independent with her own parliament.) Graham knew Burns well enough to understand how seriously to take these loyal protestations, but they were sufficient to satisfy the inquisition. It was, no doubt, as part of the same insurance policy that Burns joined the Dumfries Volunteers on 31 January 1795 and wrote their anthem, "Does Haughty Gaul Invasion Threat?" with the lines:

> Be Britain still to Britain true,
> Amang ourselves united

There have been people who have seized on these prudent insincerities to try to represent Burns as a pillar of the establishment. These were the grounds for Hugh MacDiarmid's complaints about the Burns Clubs, which he thought had done precisely that. It may have been so in the 30s when MacDiarmid wrote his celebrated essay on the subject; but I think that there is now a much more realistic appreciation of Burns's egalitarianism and nationalism. Perhaps we are now beginning to respond to the call with which MacDiarmid ended his essay:

Burns knew what he was doing when he repudiated all the canting Anglicisers and reverted to the Scots tongue and the Scots spirit. The need to follow his lead at long last is today a thousand times greater than when he gave it. We can, if we will. We can still rescue Scotland from the crash of England's collapse and the ruins of an Empire vitiated by England's infernal Ascendancy policy. We can still affirm the fearless radical spirit of the true Scotland. We can even yet throw off the yoke of all the canting humbug in our midst.[13]

References

Abbreviations
Critical Heritage: Robert Burns: the Critical Heritage, ed. Donald A Low
(London 1974)
Critical Essays: Critical Essays on Robert Burns, ed. Donald A Low
(London 1975)

[1]   James Boswell, *The Life of Samuel Johnson* (Everyman's Library,
         London 1935).

[2]   Thomas Carlyle, essay in *Edinburgh Review* (December 1828: in
         Critical Heritage, p372).

[3]   Murray Pittock, *The Invention of Scotland* (London 1991),
         pp81-83.

[4]   Tom Crawford, *Burns: A Study of the Poems and Songs*
         (Edinburgh 1994); David Murison, *Critical Essays*, p68.

[5]   David Daiches, *Critical Essays* p143.

[6]   George Rosie: (i) article in *The Herald*, 22 July 1995; (ii) Hugh
         Millar: *Outrage and an Order* (Edinburgh 1981), pp154-5.

[7]   Murray Pittock, *op.cit.* pp.79, 153.

[8]   Sir Walter Scott, unsigned review in *Quarterly Review* (February
         1809: in *Critical Heritage*, p203).

[9]   Andrew Noble in *Burns Now*, ed. Kenneth Simpson (Edinburgh
         1994).

[10]   Henry Mackenzie, unsigned essay in *The Lounger* (9 December
         1786: in *Critical Heritage*, p69).

[11]   R L Stevenson, "Some Aspects of Robert Burns", in *Familiar
         Studies of Men and Books* (Everyman's edition, London, undated),
         p168. Cedric Thorpe Davie, *Critical Essays*, p157.

[12]   Alexander Scott, *Critical Essays* p103.

[13]   Hugh MacDiarmid, "The Burns Cult", *At the Sign of the Thistle*
         (1934): in *Hugh MacDiarmid: Selected Prose*, ed. Alan Riach
         (Manchester 1992).

Scotland's Debt to Walter Scott

Address to the Edinburgh Sir Walter Scott Club, March 1996

I am very conscious of the honour of being asked to address you this evening as your President. It is also a very real pleasure to talk about Sir Walter Scott because his work has been for me a close and rewarding interest and pleasure for almost as long as I can remember. My first substantial purchase of books was a handsome set of the Melrose edition of the Waverley novels, which I bought, or persuaded my mother to buy, at an auction sale in a house in Portobello. They cost ten shillings and I was about ten years old at the time. Growing up in Edinburgh, and, like the young Walter Scott himself, going to the High School, was an experience which made you feel close to him. We were not allowed to forget it. I remember that one of our school masters in a moment of not unnatural exasperation accused the class of failing to live up to the inspiration of his example, a formidable challenge indeed.

The more you read Scott, and especially the letters and the Journal, the more he feels like a personal friend. Last autumn, you remember, this club was addressed by John Sutherland, the author of the most recent and a rather sceptical, almost hostile, biography. I had an opportunity to speak to him afterwards. I told him that my impression of his book was that he started with the idea of demolishing a legend, but that as he read into the subject he found himself liking and admiring Scott. He agreed that was precisely his experience.

It would be easy to produce long lists of people from many countries who have expressed enthusiasm for the man and his work: Goethe, Balzac, Pushkin, Manzoni, Byron and so forth. For about a hundred years he was the most popular, admired, imitated and influential writer in the world. This wide-spread popularity is by no means dead. Not long ago at a conference of International PEN I met a Hungarian who had written a book about Scott and was working on a new series of translations. At a time, a few years ago when *glasnost* was first penetrating the Soviet Union, Frank Dunlop invited

a party of their theatre directors, critics, editors and the like to come and
speak at a conference during an Edinburgh Festival. One of them, the editor
of a literary magazine with an enormous circulation, told us that he had
conducted a poll among his readers to discover what books they would
most like to see in new editions. Walter Scott was the clear winner.

Another of Scott's admirers was the great English novelist, George Eliot.
In *Middlemarch*, one of the characters is described as "reading aloud from
that beloved writer who has made a chief part in the happiness of many
young lives. The volume was *Ivanhoe*". In one of her letters in August
1871 Eliot said: "I like to tell you that my worship for Scott is peculiar ...
No other writer would serve as a substitute ... It is a personal grief, a heart-
wound to me when I hear a depreciating or slighting word about Scott."

I feel rather like that myself and I know that many of us do. When
George Eliot wrote these words, I do not suppose that there many
depreciating or slighting words to trouble her; but if there was a trickle
then, it has become a flood. It has become a commonplace, and strangely
enough especially here in his own Scotland, for people who should know
better to dismiss Scott with a contemptuous sneer. Very often there is good
reason to suppose that the people who do this are merely following fashion
and have hardly read Scott, if at all. The aspects on which he is most criticised
are among those for which he was most praised in the past, the effect of his
work on the understanding of history in general and of that of Scotland in
particular and on attitudes towards Scotland both among ourselves and in
the world at large. It is this astonishing reversal of opinion that I should
like to consider tonight.

Of course, there were those who disagreed with Scott, even during his
own life-time. James Hogg, John Galt and Thomas McCrie thought that
Scott in *Old Mortality* had been unfair to the Covenanters, although he
responded with a spirited defence. Hogg, who knew Scott well, said that
the only foible that he could ever discover in his character was "a too strong
leaning to the old aristocracy of the country". Lockhart in effect agrees but
offers an explanation: "a historical name was a charm that literally stirred
his blood. But not so a mere title." On the other hand, Lockhart also tells us
of an estate worker at Abbotsford who said, "Sir Walter speaks to every
man as if they were blood relations." I do not think that he could have
written the novels if that were not so, because they depend on a deep
understanding of people of all classes and descriptions. The best passages

are in the Scots speech of ordinary men and women, and they, like Jeannie Deans and Edie Ochiltree, are among the most admirable characters. This was, I think, entirely conscious and deliberate on Scott's part. Lockhart, for once, tells a story against himself when Scott reproved him for an apparently condescending remark and said, "I have read books enough, and observed and conversed with enough of eminent and splendidly cultivated minds too, in my time; but I assure you, I have heard higher sentiments from the lips of poor uneducated men and women ... than I have ever yet met with out of the pages of the Bible."

Scott's first biographer, George Allan, who published a *Life* in 1834, noted this contradiction between Scott's weakness for the old aristocracy and the fact that his heart, as he says, was "evidently with the great mass of society". This contradiction extended to Scott's political allegiance, of which Allan clearly disapproved. "Scott," he wrote, "had thrown himself, with the blind vehemence of youth, into the ranks of the British Tories, the most narrow-minded politicians of the age. Dogged adherence to what was established, be it right or wrong, deep, bitter and enduring hatred of every opponent, was what they required".

Scott, as one of my predecessors in this place, Malcolm Rifkind, reminded us three years ago, certainly regarded himself as a Tory. He explained this with disarming frankness in one of his letters to Anna Seward:

I was not only very early disposed to what have been called Tory principles by the opinion of those whom I respected and was brought up to respect but the favours I received, the intimacy in which I lived with many of Lord Melville's family ... was founded as much upon attachment to their measures in 1792-3 as to gratitude for favours received at a time when they were truly valuable.

Of course this Tory party was something very different from the Tory party of today. It had started as the party of the Jacobites and of the opponents of the Union of 1707. By Scott's time, it had become a machine to retain political support by means of appointments and other favours. In that respect, perhaps things are still much the same. Unlike the modern party, however, it was highly resistant to any change in the established order. Scott was generally in sympathy with that both by instinct and philosophy, although he was also fascinated by the new. I think that it was Virginia Woolf who remarked that he may have been the Last Minstrel, but he was also the first chairman of the Edinburgh Oil Gas Company.

The other points in George Allan's description of the Tories do not apply to Scott at all. He was certainly not narrow-minded and hatred was alien to his nature. In the same letter to Anna Seward he went on to say: "I am candid enough to esteem the principles and cherish the friendship of many whose political opinions are different from my own, because I know they are adopted ... from an internal conviction." When it came to a question of the interest of Scotland, he was always in favour of all parties standing together, as he advocated in the *Malachi* letters. "So Tory and Whig", he wrote in his Journal on 21 January 1826, "may go be damned together, as names that have disturbed old Scotland, and torn asunder the most kindly feelings since the first day they were invented." Lockhart in the conclusion of his biography summed up Scott's political feelings in these words:

> The love of his country became indeed a passion...he would have bled and died to preserve even the airiest surviving nothing of her antique pretensions for Scotland...Whenever Scotland could be considered as standing separate on any question from the rest of the empire, he was not only apt, but eager to embrace the opportunity of again rehoisting, as it were, the old signal of national independence.

Scott himself, in language very reminiscent of Robert Burns, spoke of his "Scottish feelings — prejudices, if you will, but which were born, and will die with me". He used another phrase of Burns when he urged Allan Cunningham to undertake more ambitious literary projects "for dear auld Scotland's sake". This was the spirit in which Burns collected Scottish songs and Scott the Border Ballads, a tribute, as he said, to a country "once proud and independent". Both Burns and Scott deeply regretted and resented the Union of 1707 and Scotland's loss of independence. Both were determined to resist, as far as they could, the erosion of the Scottish identity. The collections of the songs and ballads were part of this resistance. So were the Waverley novels and, more obviously and politically, the *Letters of Malachi Malagrowther*. "I shall always be proud of *Malachi*", Scott wrote in his Journal on 9 June 1826, "as having headed back the Southron, or helped to do so, in one instance at least".

Burns and Scott agreed too in their understanding of the means by which the Union was brought about. Burns in

> We're bought and sold for English gold,
> Such a parcel of rogues in a nation!

— Scott in the chapter on the Union in his *Tales of a Grandfather* where the strength of his feelings are clear from the vigour and passion of the language. The Scottish nation, he says, regarded the Union as a "total surrender of their independence, by their false and corrupted statesmen...despised by the English and detested by their own country". He asks whether the "descendants of the noble lords and honourable gentlemen", who accepted the bribes, "would be more shocked at the general fact of their ancestors being corrupted, or scandalised at the paltry amount of the bribe". In the whole of the 19th century this chapter is virtually the only honest account of the Union transaction. In that century of the British Empire, anything which questioned or discredited the Union was unwelcome and by general consent suppressed. This is why this aspect of Burns and Scott has been largely forgotten.

It was not so in Scott's own time. When Robert Peel walked up the High Street of Edinburgh in August 1822 through the crowd gathered for the royal visit, he said that Scott was everywhere recognised and the reaction of the people first gave him a notion of the "electric shock of a nation's gratitude". The same word was used by Lord Meadowbank at the dinner in the Assembly Rooms in George Street at which Scott first publicly acknowledged that he had written the Waverley novels. "We owe to him, as a people," Meadowbank said, "a large and heavy debt of gratitude." And he explained why. It was due to Scott that the fame of our ancestors who fought for independence and liberty was no longer confined to Scotland. "He it is who has conferred a new reputation on our national character, and bestowed on Scotland an imperishable name."

Lockhart in *Peter's Letters to his Kinsfolk* said much the same. The generation of Hume and Smith had produced a literature of powerful thought but it had ignored Scottish history, the national character, poetry and feeling. "The folly of slighting and concealing what remains concealed within herself," Lockhart continued, "is one of the worst and most pernicious that can beset a country." Scott had ended this. He had grappled boldly with the feelings of his countrymen. He was, Lockhart concluded, "the sole saviour of all the richer and warmer spirit of literature in Scotland". Of course, Scott was not alone. Ramsay, Fergusson, Burns and, in Scott's own generation, Galt and Hogg, and many others, all made valiant contributions. A nation which loses control over its own affairs depends for its survival on its musicians and artists, but above all on its writers. Scotland has been fortunate in this respect and among them Scott has been an influence of prodigious force. It is wholly appropriate that in Princes Street he has the grandest monument ever erected to a literary man.

The theme of gratitude to Scott for his contribution to Scotland has continued. When Lord Cockburn heard of his death he wrote in his Journal: "Scotland never owed so much to one man." Several of my distinguished predecessors have noted their agreement. Harold Macmillan: "For Scotland, he achieved two great ends. He made her people and her history known in every part of the civilised world. In addition, he made Scotland known to herself." Alexander Gray: "What Scotland owes to Burns and Scott is beyond all computation."

We cannot say that this is still the universal view. I am not speaking about his literary reputation either among readers or critics. In such a matter there are fluctuations of fashion and taste. Hugh Walpole in the *Times Literary Supplement* of 3 April 1938 said that Scott's "glorious position" in critical estimation had lasted for more than 70 years until the early 1900s; but that in 1938 he occupied "a lowlier place than will ever be his again". Walpole was probably thinking of the notorious passage in E. M. Foster's *Aspects of the Novel*, first published in 1928, where he said that Scott had "a trivial mind and a heavy style. He cannot construct. He has neither artistic detachment or passion, and how can a writer who is devoid of both, create characters who will move us deeply?" I am willing to concede that Scott sometimes in English, but never in Scots, has a heavy style; but all the other points are the opposite of the truth. I need not detain you in replying to any of this because that has been done to great effect by many writers, David Cecil, Donald Davie, Virginia Woolf, Duncan Forbes and above all by another of my predecessors, David Daiches. His brilliant essay, "Scott's Achievement as a Novelist", first published in 1951, has done more than anything else to re-establish in the highest rank of critical esteem the nine novels set in Scotland in the 100 years or so before Scott's own time:

Waverley, Guy Mannering, The Antiquary, Old Mortality, The Heart of Midlothian, Rob Roy, The Bride of Lammermoor, The Legend of Montrose and *Redgauntlet*.

What I want to discuss is something rather different: why is it that the qualities in Scott which excited the gratitude of his countrymen in the past now seem to be disregarded or forgotten? I take as an example the following passage from the recently published *Encyclopaedia of Scotland*, edited by John and Julia Keay:

> Regarded in his own day as one of the greatest of writers, and rewarded with great wealth and a baronetcy, he was later seen as venal, and his successive novels merely romances, repetitiously reworking established motifs and perpetuating deluding myths about Scottish history and nationhood.

Unfortunately they do not tell us what myths they have in mind. To be fair to them, I do not think that the editors intend this to be a statement of their own view, but as a summary of the current attitude among the public at large. If they are even approximately right, it is clear that the public have been very badly misled. The allegation about venality is a red herring which it is not worth while to pursue; but the points about history go to the heart of the matter.

One of the earliest references which I have come across to the idea that Scott's influence had been harmful and not beneficial was from an unexpected source, a lecture which W. P. Ker gave at the Sorbonne in May 1919. He said that there were those who suspect and blame Scott's work because "it is reactionary, illiberal, and offensive to modern ideas of progress". The spokesman of this party, he said, was Mark Twain and he referred to Twain's *Life on the Mississippi*, which was published in 1882. This is the book in which Twain denounced Scott for impeding the ideas of the French Revolution of "liberty, humanity and progress" by injecting what he calls "Walter Scott Middle-Age sham civilisation". He says that Scott "had so large a hand in making the Southern character" of the United States that he was "in great measure" responsible for the Civil War. This was all due to what he called the "pernicious" effects of *Ivanhoe*, a single book which had done as much harm as *Don Quixote* had done good. This is the allegation of the harmful influence of false history at its most extreme, but

Twain does not refer to Scotland and the recent past, but to *Ivanhoe* and the Middle Ages. Even so, I suspect that many people were influenced directly or indirectly by denunciations like this and assumed that it applied to the whole of Scott's work.

Ivor Brown in a book published in 1952 said that if it was true that "nobody reads Scott nowadays", the fault lay largely in the class-room. He said that the wrong books were chosen and they were wrongly used. The books he mentions were *Ivanhoe* again, *The Talisman*, *Woodstock* and *Quentin Durward*. Any writer who writes a great deal produces work which is not equal to his best. As we all know, Scott's later novels were produced under great pressure and were far from his best. Virtually all contemporary critics agree that his finest novels are the nine set in Scotland and in the recent past. They are also, as it happens, those where Scott made a positive contribution to our understanding, not only of the Scottish past, but of the nature of the historical process. They are novels and not history, but they give not only a vivid, but a fair and penetrating, view of Scottish life at their time. Nothing could be further from deluding myth. It may be that some people have turned away from these nine novels because the best passages are in Scots. I remember reading an essay by V. S. Pritchett in which he said that English distaste for Scottish speech had finally hardened into complete rejection. If that is so, they are missing a lot. In Scotland we are more fortunate because the Scots language is in itself a source of a particular pleasure which no other language can provide for us.

Some great historians have spoken very highly of Scott's influence on the understanding and writing of history. Thomas Carlyle, for instance:

> These historical Novels have taught all men this truth, which looks like a truism, and yet was as good as unknown to writers of history and others, till so taught: that the bygone ages of the world were actually filled by living men, not by protocols, state-papers, controversies and abstractions of men... History will henceforth have to take thought of it... It is a great service fertile in consequences, this that Scott has done; a great truth laid open by him.

And G. M. Trevelyan:

> He did more than any professional historian to make mankind advance

towards a true conception of history, for it was he who first perceived that the history of mankind is not simple but complex, that history never repeats itself but ever creates new forms differing according to time and place.

Walter Bagehot commented on Scott's grasp of economics and in particular on the account of economic conditions in both the Highlands and the Borders which is to be found in the novels. He said that they showed a "digested accuracy and theoretical completeness" and that "you might cut paragraphs, even from his lighter writings, which would be thought acute in the *Wealth of Nations*".

Statements like these are impressive support for the view that Scott, so far from distorting our ideas of the past, in fact enlarged and deepened it. Those who tell us that Scott constructed "deluding myths" about the Scottish past are seldom specific, with a few exceptions. He is accused, as though it were a crime, of persuading the whole of Scotland to adopt tartan and the pipes as national symbols. There is some truth in this because of the effect of the visit of George IV in 1822, which Scott stage-managed, and where Highland chiefs and tartan played a very large part. So Scott was guilty in this respect, but guilty of a very important achievement. The tartan and the pipes are wonderful and potent symbols which we should cherish. They also mark the reconciliation of the Lowlands and the Highlands, which, to quote Trevelyan again, has united us in a common national pride ever since the days of Sir Walter Scott.

Another, and more serious charge is that Scott took an essentially defeatist view of the Scottish past, summed up in Redgauntlet's famous remark at the end of the novel that the cause was lost for ever. Hugh MacDiarmid discusses this idea in his book *Lucky Poet*, although he blames critics like Herbert Grierson and Edwin Muir rather than Scott himself. MacDiarmid also recognised, inconsistently perhaps, that Scott's resistance to Anglicisation "leads on naturally", as he said, "to the separatist position". Recently the theory of defeatism has been more fully developed by Murray Pittock in his book, *The Invention of Scotland*. He suggests that Scott deliberately made use of the theme of Jacobitism because its defeat "could be conveniently conflated with the defeat of Scotland as a whole". He says that Scott loved Scotland but only if it was safely confined to the past. There have been one or two other similar theories. Nicolas Phillipson, to my mind distorting the evidence, has suggested that Scott transformed Scottish nationalism into "an ideology of noisy inaction". Colin Kidd said in a recent book that Scott realised "that civil peace and social harmony depended upon defusing the Nation's past". None of these assertions are supported by very much by way of argument or illustration.

I must say of all such theories that the authors of them have an idea of the character of Walter Scott very different from my own if they can believe that he was capable of anything so Machiavellian, devious and anti-Scottish and without a word about it in his letters or Journal. Scott was a Jacobite partly, as he says himself, because of family tradition, and partly for the reason which he ascribed to Robert Burns: no "youth of warm imagination and ardent patriotism brought up in Scotland" at that time could be anything else. Jacobitism was an expression of Scottish patriotism and of a desire to escape from the Union. Of course Scott realised that it was dead as a practical policy of restoring the Stewarts to the throne. In that sense, the cause was indeed lost for ever; but the cause of Scotland was not lost and Scott was determined to devote his talents and energy to fighting for it. If you are in any doubt about that, you need only read the first two *Letters of Malachi Malagrowther*, which are among the most passionate statements ever written of the value of the Scottish identity and the need to assert it. Let me end by reading just three or four sentences from the first:

> What are we esteemed by the English? Wretched drivellers, incapable of understanding our own affairs; or greedy peculators, unfit to be trusted? On what ground are we considered either as the one or the other? ... For God's sake, sir, let us remain as nature made us, Englishmen, Irishmen and Scotchmen, with something like the impress of our several countries upon each!

The literary critics have restored Scott's literary reputation. I think that it is time now to re-assess his great contribution, not only to the understanding, but to the survival, of Scotland as a nation. I am sure that this will lead to the conclusion that Lord Cockburn was right when he said that Scotland never owed so much to one man.

In that spirit, I ask you to drink to the memory of Sir Walter Scott.

SOME CONSEQUENCES

A Personal Note

The following was written in 1987 as the opening section of an essay, The Need for Independence. For reasons of space, it was omitted when the piece was published in the Glasgow Herald of 6 June 1987 and subsequently reprinted in my book, Towards Independence (Polygon, 1991 and 1996). These opening pages are now published for the first time.

The circumstances of my life have given me the chance to observe and consider Scotland both from within and without. I was brought up in Edinburgh and had the good fortune (which Scottish education denies to most people) to discover Scottish history and literature quite early in life. I have never stopped reading and studying them, but much of my life has been spent abroad. I went straight from the University to the army during the war. At the end of it, I was in Berlin and was persuaded to take the Foreign Office examination. Although, in consequence, I was moving about the world for about the next 30 years, I never lost touch with Scotland. Wherever I went, I took a fairly substantial collection of Scottish books; I managed to get back nearly every year for at least a week or two. Indeed it is possible that I saw Scotland in sharper focus just because I was so often on the outside. Life as a diplomat has many disadvantages, but it does give you a ring-side seat to observe the affairs of other countries, and comparisons are inescapable. The more I learned about other countries, the more I was struck by the anomalies which afflict Scotland. There are few, if any, places where the case for self-government is so compelling and where the standard of living and quality of life are so far below their potential.

The small independent countries of Western Europe, such as Norway, Denmark, Austria and Switzerland, are closely comparable to Scotland in size, climate and general historical development. All have left Scotland far behind, both in material prosperity and other less tangible satisfactions. Take, for example, Switzerland, which is one which I happen to know well. Switzerland is smaller than Scotland in area but her population is now larger. Nearly all the natural advantages are in Scotland's favour. Switzerland is land-locked, not surrounded by sea which is rich in fish and oil. It is even more mountainous than Scotland and has no coal or other minerals. You would therefore expect to find Scotland much more prosperous than Switzerland. In fact, it is precisely the opposite. The Swiss GNP per head is more than twice as high as our own and their unemployment is a mere fraction. That is only part of it. I think that it is obvious as you travel around Switzerland that it is a society visibly more flourishing, content and self-assured than our own.

A comparison with any of these small countries of Western Europe would lead to the same conclusion. Their standards of living are among the highest in the world. They are not only prosperous, but socially harmonious and self-confident. In E. F. Schumacher's famous phrase, "small is beautiful". But it seems that political independence, control of their own affairs, is an essential prerequisite. Without it, Scotland is simply not in the same league and this is painfully obvious by almost any standard of measurement. Take, for instance, the public health statistics. Scotland is the least healthy country in Europe in everything from dental decay to cancer. How has this come about in a country that has contributed probably more than any other to the development of modern medical science?

As Adam Smith remarked, "the most decisive mark of the prosperity of any country is the increase of the number of its inhabitants". Alone among Western European countries, Scotland has been losing population. The Registrar General has estimated officially that we shall lose a further half million over the next 40 years. This is consistent, of course, with the erosion of industry in Scotland and the steady loss of control over the industries and financial institutions that still remain. In the 1930s Edwin Muir said that his main impression of Scotland was that it was "gradually being emptied of its population, its spirit, its wealth, industry, art, intellect and innate character". It was defenceless because it had no centre to hold it together as an organic society. That is still the position and in many ways the decline has accelerated, especially in the last few years.

The malaise and decline in Scotland cannot be explained by lack of natural resources. With coal, oil, agriculture and fish, we are in a much more favourable position that most of the comparable countries in Europe. Nor does history suggest that our people are deficient in intelligence, skill, enterprise and endeavour. On the contrary, the record of Scottish achievement is almost without parallel among countries of its size. This is true not only of philosophy and literature but of science and technology as well. Apart from the great names, countless Scots have made important contributions to the development of other countries in every corner of the world. That Scotland itself has provided fewer opportunities for the exercise of their energies and talents is another symptom that something is fundamentally wrong.

In some strange way, Scotland has been left aside by one of the great tendencies of the 20th century, the movement towards self-determination. Two world wars have been fought in defence of this principle. After the first, several European states emerged from the dissolution of the Austro-Hungarian Empire. The second was followed by the massive movement of decolonisation. From the former British Empire alone, 39 countries with a combined population of over 900 million obtained their independence. There has been a steady increase in the number of independent countries. The old League of Nations was founded in 1920 with 41 member countries. When the United Nations was founded in 1945 it had 51 members; it now has 159. The principle of self-determination was embodied in the Charter of the United Nations. It was reaffirmed in 1975 in the Final Act of the Helsinki Conference where it was defined in these terms:

> By virtue of the principle of equal rights and self-determination of peoples, all peoples always have the right, in full freedom, to determine, when and as they wish, their internal and external political status, without external interference, and to pursue as they wish their political, economic, social and cultural development.

The United Kingdom and all other countries of Europe, as well as Canada and the United States, were signatories of that Final Act. They included countries as small as Liechtenstein, Luxembourg, Malta and Monaco, but not Scotland. For the Scottish people are clearly not free, at present, "to pursue as they wish their political, economic, social and cultural development". That, I think, is the basic cause of our present malaise. We need self-determination as much as any other people, and have no less right to it.

Many of the countries which have become independent in the last forty years are smaller than Scotland and poorer in natural resources. Most of them had no previous experience of self-government and were critically short of personnel educated for administration or the professions. Scotland, on the other hand, has been exporting trained administrators, teachers, doctors, bankers and engineers for centuries. We have a long history of independent government and can, indeed, claim to have invented the idea of self-determination with the Declaration of Arbroath of 1320. We successfully defended our independence for over 300 years in the longest war in European history. It is therefore very strange that, in the general movement towards self-determination and decolonisation, Scotland of all places should be left behind as a sort of relic of colonialism. In the heyday of the British Empire, when it was the strongest and richest of world powers, Scotland was a partner in the management. We paid a price for this in the neglect of our own affairs and in a disproportionate tribute of blood to the army. In the past, the Empire provided an opportunity for individual Scots to make careers for themselves overseas. Now we have declined into a subordinate position without any compensating advantage. We have less autonomy than the Isle of Man or the Channel Islands. When Malcolm Rifkind was Secretary of State for Scotland he was quite right to describe himself as a colonial Governor-General.

Some of the newly independent countries have suffered natural or man-made misfortunes of various kinds, but none of them doubt that they have benefited from independence. None would be willing to give it up. Independence has brought self-respect, the release of creative energy, increased prosperity, new opportunities and an enhanced quality of life. Scotland, with its resources and its education and skilled population, would benefit even more dramatically.

"A severed and withered branch"
The Rise and Fall of Britishness

Paper for 4th International Symposium,
University of Mainz at Germersheim, October, 1994.

The first part of the title which I have given to this paper comes from a remark by Hume Brown, the author of a history of Scotland which was standard work on the subject for about the first half of this century. In a book which he edited in 1907 he said this about the loss of our own distinct monarchy in 1603 when James VI succeeded also to the throne of England:

> The Union of the Crowns brought many disadvantages to Scotland, but the result of it that most vitally affected her was her severance from the nations at a period when new principles and new ideas were guiding their policy. Throughout the entire century Scotland was a severed and withered branch, and her people know it.[1]

It is a recognition of the importance of the links between Scotland and the rest of Europe that Hume Brown should regard their severance as the most serious consequence of 1603. There were many others which were also very damaging. With the King went the control of foreign policy, the executive direction of the government, appointments to all state offices, patronage of the arts. In all these matters the King now acted on the advice of English ministers. Scottish foreign trade was sacrificed in the interest of English policy. Scotland contributed men and money to the prosecution of English wars, but was ignored in the peace settlements and was deprived of all capacity to defend herself. Succession to the wealth, strength and remoteness of England meant an enormous increase in the personal power of the King. In the words of William Robertson, "the Kings of Scotland, once the most limited, became, in an instant, the most absolute Princes in Europe".[2] The civil wars of the 17th century were one of the consequences.

The Revolution of 1688-9 restored to the Scottish Parliament the freedom to discuss and decide as it pleased, but otherwise the royal restrictions on

Scottish autonomy remained. All state appointments still remained in the hands of the absentee King in London and all legislation required his assent. The Parliament elected in 1703, to the limited extent that Parliaments were then elected, devoted itself for the next four years to this problem of indirect English control. It began by a robust assertion of Scottish independence for the first two years by passing in both 1703 and 1704 the Act of Security which provided for either the reversion to a separate monarchy or the transfer of all power from the monarch to Parliament. It ended in 1707 by voting itself out of existence and accepting an incorporating union with England. As Murray Pittock has said, these two Acts were "the last constitutional threats to English domination of the British Isles, and the Union was the means to end their challenge".[3]

How this came about I have attempted to explain in my books on the Union and on Andrew Fletcher. For the moment let me summarise with drastic brevity. The Union was vastly unpopular in Scotland. It was more an imposition than an agreement and it was achieved by bribery and other inducements with the implied threat of military force in the background. My present subject is not the Union itself, but the various ways in which the Scottish people have reacted to it in the three centuries which have followed.

When the Union was under discussion the Church historian, Robert Wodrow, said in a letter in May 1706:

I have a great many melancholy thoughts of living to see this antient Kingdome made a province, and not only our religiouse and civil liberty lost, but lost irrevocably, and this is the most dismall aspect ane incorporating union has to me, that it putts matters past help...once lost, ever lost.[4]

A pamphlet of 1706, *State of the Controversy Betwixt United and Separate Parliaments*, which may have been written in part by Andrew Fletcher, made the same point:

This will be the Issue of that darling Plea, of being one and not two; it will be turned upon the Scots with a Vengeance; and their 45 Scots Members may dance round to all Eternity, in this trap of their own making.[5]

The truth of this was soon demonstrated. Even the Scottish lords who had been most active in the ratification of the Treaty of Union regretted it within a few years and moved for its repeal in the House of Lords. They failed there by a few votes, but there was no possibility of success in the Commons where the Scots were a small minority.

In Bruce Lenman's words: "After 1707 only force could reverse the decision that the English state should absorb Scotland, and only Jacobites were prepared to give a lead in resorting to force to break the Union." [6] This posed a hopeless dilemma. Most Scots, in the Lowlands at least, were opposed to Jacobitism because it implied arbitrary monarchy and Catholicism or Episcopalianism. They were also opposed to the Union; but they could see no way to escape it without bloodshed, confusion and the probability that even worse terms would be imposed on them at the end.

The general reaction to the Union in Scotland, in contrast to the rejoicing in England, was one of benumbed dismay. The people, the Earl of Mar (who was one of the chief promoters of the Union) told Queen Anne in a letter of June 1708, "are mightily sour'd".[7] For decades, the economy and everything else were in stagnation and decline. Scotland was not only more "severed and withered" than before, but ignored even by the Government in London, apart from the ruthless suppression of the Highlands after the '45. As the people tried to come to terms with this unhappy situation, two opposite responses appeared. One was to accept the unalterable and make the best of it by trying to become as English as possible. The other was a determination to resist assimilation by preserving and emphasising Scottishness in spite of the humiliation of the Union. These opposite tendencies can be seen, not only between different people, but even within the same individual, a state described by David Daiches as cultural schizophrenia.[8] Allan Ramsay (1684-1758) was one of the first and most obvious examples of the condition. In 1712 he founded the Easy Club for convivial discussion of literature and politics. The members adopted pseudonyms. Ramsay first took Isaac Bickerstaff to show his admiration for the Augustan wits of London and then changed to Gavin Douglas to proclaim his Scottish patriotism. So it was in his own poetry, resorting sometimes to painful English imitation, but more often to Scots. He argued for the use of the Scots tongue and published anthologies of the mediaeval makars. In one of them he attributed two poems in favour of Scottish independence to Alexander Scott but they were almost certainly by himself. Since power and patronage were in the hands of the unionist establishment, there were risks in speaking against it. Daiches[9] says that Ramsay did not dare to write in his own name against the Union, but that is not quite true. He did so in a poem of 1724, but it was not published in his own lifetime and the dreaded word, Union, is indicated only by its initial.

James Boswell (1740-1795) is the most illuminating case study, if only because no one else has left us such a detailed account of his thoughts and feelings. He started to make his way as an advocate in Edinburgh, with every prospect of becoming a judge like his father; he was the heir to one of the most beautiful country houses in Scotland; he was on familiar terms with Hume, Kames and other great men of the Scottish Enlightenment; on the testimony of Franklin, Amyat and many others, conversation and conviviality in Edinburgh was as agreeable and civilised as you could find anywhere. With all these advantages, Boswell pined throughout his life for the delights of London and eventually moved himself and his family there with unhappy consequences.

He was constantly torn in two directions. When he was in Holland in 1764 he proposed to compile a dictionary of Scots because, "the Scottish language is being lost every day and in a short time will become quite unintelligible. To me, who have the true patriotic soul of an old Scotsman, that would seem a pity."[10] But he frequently expresses disgust with Edinburgh manners, "its narrow sphere", "vulgar jocularity" and "forward vulgarity".[11] At one moment in December 1785, "the idea of making my children *alien* from Scotland was dismal"; but at another in July 1789, "were my daughters to be *Edinburgh-mannered girls*, I could have no satisfaction in their company".[12]

In spite of this vacillation about Scottish manners and the Scottish tongue, Boswell was consistent in his opposition to the Union. In December 1764 he records the following conversation with Rousseau: "BOSWELL: Since our cursed Union. ROUSSEAU: You undid yourselves. BOSWELL: Truly yes". Boswell then promises to provide Rousseau with anecdotes and details about the making of the Union for a biography of Fletcher of Saltoun and says that he will do this "with the warmth of an ancient Scot".[13] In August 1773, when Boswell took Johnson to visit the Parliament House in Edinburgh, he expressed "a warm regret, that, by our Union with England, we were no more; — our independent Kingdom was lost". James Kerr, the Keeper of the Records, added, "Half our nation was bribed by English money." "Sir," said Johnson, "that is no defence: that makes you worse."[14]

Towards the end of his life in London in 1790 Boswell recorded in his *Journal* that he "attacked the Union and said the nation was gone".[15]

Schizophrenia could hardly go further. There were no doubt particular reasons why Boswell was so susceptible to the pull of London. As the seat of the royal court and government and therefore of power, wealth, fame and fashion, London was irresistible then, and to some people still, and especially to the snobbish and socially or politically ambitious. Boswell was susceptible to all of these temptations. For him it was associated with the pleasures to which he had escaped from the censorious eyes of his father. The particular problem of Scottish speech was one which Boswell shared with many of his contemporaries, even Hume. Eighteenth-century ideas about refinement, combined with ignorance of the history of the language, made it easy to suppose that Scots was no more than a debased form of English. From despising the language it was a short step to despising those who spoke it.

But Boswell had also rationalised his feelings. He disliked the Union, but he drew rational conclusions about its consequences. Since Edinburgh was no longer a seat of government, it offered insufficient scope for the ambitious. He wrote in his Journal on 23 March 1783: "I am clearly persuaded that a man of my family, talents, and connexions may reasonably endeavour to be employed in a more elevated sphere than in Scotland, now that it is in reality only a province."[16] He developed the thought in a letter to a London newspaper in April 1779:

> Since the Union of the two Kingdoms, which deprived us of all national dignity and all the advantages of a vice-court and of a parliament in our own district, London is now the metropolis of the whole island, the grand emporium of everything valuable, the strong centre of attraction for all of us.[17]

That is a reasonable explanation; but the contradictions, inhibitions and embarrassments, which are so obvious in most 18th century Scottish comment about the Union, may reflect darker emotions. Hume Brown suggested that the Scots had "averted their gaze" from the way in which the Union came about by "unconscious instinct", because it "compromised the national character in the eyes of the world".[18] In other words, it was too shameful to be faced. More recently William Wolfe, who was Chairman of the SNP from 1969 to 1979, has suggested that the Scots are politically inhibited by repressed emotions of shame, guilt, anger and fear because of the eclipse of Scotland without a struggle in 1707.[19] Such theories are impossible to prove or disprove, of course; but they do offer an explanation of much that is mysterious in this whole matter.

Contradiction and confusion are perhaps to be expected from an insecure character like James Boswell, but the solid and lucid intellect of David Hume provides a more surprising example. The attitude to England which he expresses in his published work is in complete contrast to the feelings revealed in his private letters. In his *Essays, Moral, Political and Literary*, he sometimes refers to himself as though he were English and he speaks very favourably of England. In "Of Refinement in the Arts" he says that an English (or French) gentleman is of "the rank of men the most civilised in the most civilised nations".[20] In "Of the Protestant Sucession" he says of Britain in the sixty years since 1688: "So long and so glorious a period no nation almost can boast of... So free, so rational, and so suitable to the dignity of human nature."[21] When you turn to the letters, it is difficult to believe that he is speaking of the same place. Some examples: "The taste for Literature is neither Decayd nor depravd here, as with the Barbarians who inhabit the Banks of the Thames" (April, 1764).[22] "I am delighted to see the daily and hourly Progress of Madness and Folly and Wickedness in England" (Oct. 1769).[23] "It has been my misfortune to write in the Language of the most stupid and factious Barbarians in the World" (Oct. 1769).[24] And as for regarding himself as English:

> I do not believe that there is one Englishman in fifty, who, if he heard that I had broke my neck tonight, would not be rejoic'd with it. Some hate me because I am not a Tory, some because I am not a Whig, some because I am not a Christian, and all because I am a Scotsman. Can you seriously talk of my continuing an Englishman? Am I, or are you, an Englishman? Will they allow us to be so? Do they not treat with Derision our Pretentions to that name, and with Hatred our just Pretensions to surpass and to govern them?[25]

Also, in his *History* Hume had debunked the central myth of English constitutional development. To quote Nicholas Phillipson:

Not only did he show that the origins of the constitution were not in the least ancient, as so many Englishmen fondly believed...but the history of England as told by Hume could hardly have been less glorious... It was the story of...ignorance, superstition and zealotry.[26]

Although you might not think so from these remarks by Hume, many people in Scotland by about 1760 regarded the Union, no longer with hostility, but with acceptance or even approval. In 1765 in Avignon Boswell told the exiled Jacobite, James Murray, that he feared that most people in Scotland were now reconciled to the Union, "because they have lost all principle and spirit of patriotism".[27] A few years earlier, in April 1760, Adam Smith in a letter to William Strahan was explicit about the change in mood:

Nothing, however, appears to me more excusable than the disaffection of Scotland at that time. [It is clear from the context that he is speaking of the years around 1707.] The Union was a measure from which infinite Good has been derived to this country. The prospect of that good, however, must then have appeared very remote and very uncertain. The immediate effect of it was to hurt the interest of every single order of men in the country. The dignity of the nobility was undone by it. The greater part of the Gentry who had been accustomed to represent their own country in its own Parliament were cut out for ever from all hopes of representing it in a British Parliament. Even the merchants seemed to suffer at first. The trade to the Plantations was, indeed, opened to them. But it was a trade which they knew nothing about: the trade they were acquainted with, that to France, Holland and the Baltic, was laid under new embarrassments which almost totally annihilated the two first and most important branches of it. The Clergy too, who were far from insignificant, were alarmed about the Church. No wonder if at the time all orders of men conspired in cursing a measure so hurtful to their immediate interest. The views of their Posterity are now very different; but those views could be seen by but few of our forefathers, by those few in but a confused and imperfect manner.[28]

In the *Wealth of Nations* (first published in 1776), Smith makes three references to the Union. He says that "of all the commercial advantages" of the Union (without specifying what they were) the "rise in the price of cattle was perhaps the greatest".[29] On the other hand: "The wool of Scotland fell very considerably in its price in consequence of the union with England, by which it was excluded from the great market of Europe, and confined to the narrow one of Great Britain." [30] The third point is not economic but political: "By the union with England the middling and inferior ranks of people in Scotland gained a complete deliverance from the power of an aristocracy which had always before oppressed them."[31] This last point (which has been taken up by some modern apologists for the Union) is not historically accurate. The heritable jurisdictions, on which the power of the aristocracy rested, were not abolished, but specifically preserved, by the Treaty of Union. In the Scottish Parliament the ratification of the Treaty largely depended on the votes of the Lords, who were unlikely to undermine themselves. The Treaty abolished their automatic right to sit in Parliament, but it gave them the other privileges of the English peers, including immunity from arrest for debt, which was of real practical advantage to many of them. In fact, the heritable jurisdictions had long largely fallen into desuetude, but they were not formally abolished until after the '45.

This point therefore suggests that Smith had fallen into the familiar fallacy of *post hoc ergo propter hoc*. The same may be true of perceptions of the economic effects. As the trading community had foreseen, and as Smith remarked in his letter to Strahan, the immediate effects of the Union on the Scottish economy were disastrous. Scotland, by her own efforts, started to recover by about the middle of the 18th century and then made rapid economic progress because of new technology in agriculture and manufacturing. Walter Scott said in his *Letters of Malachi Malagrowther*, "Scotland... was left from the year 1750 under the guardianship of her own institutions, to win her silent way to national wealth and consequence."[32] He went on to say that between the American war and the time when he was writing in 1826, the prosperity of Scotland had increased in a ratio five times greater than that of England. Since this great increase in wealth followed the Union, even after a long interval, it may well have been given the credit which was in fact due to the new technologies.

Not that every one was taken in. It was in the 1770s that Robert Fergusson wrote:

> Black be the day that e'er to England's ground
> Scotland was eikit by the Union's bond. [33]

About twenty years later Robert Burns said in a letter to Mrs. Dunlop: "Alas, have I often said to myself, what are all the boased advantages which my country reaps from a certain Union, that can counterbalance the annihilation of her Independence, and even her very name?" [34]

At about the same time the great men of the Scottish Enlightenment were writing on history and philosophy. Much of their work considered the process of social change, of which you might suppose that Scotland since the Union was an illuminating example. Even when they probably had it in mind, they tended to draw their examples from classical Greece and Rome or from the Indians of North America. This was probably politically prudent, because they were, after all, close to the '45. However, I am struck by the number of suggestions, scattered through their work, that they hankered after the independence of a small nation and believed in the virtues of cultural diversity. David Hume in his essay, "The Idea of a Perfect Commonwealth", says that "a small commonwealth is the happiest government in the world within itself, because every thing lies under the eyes of the rulers".[35] In "Of the Rise of the Arts and Sciences," he says that "divisions into small states are favourable to learning, by stopping the progress of authority as well as that of power," and he goes on to cite the example of the Greek city states.[36] All of this is very reminiscent of Andrew Fletcher. There is a consistent line of thought in Scotland from Fletcher to Hume and Scott's *Malachi* and to the writers of the present century in favour of cultural diversity and the independence of small nations.

There are similar thoughts in Adam Ferguson and Adam Smith. In his *Essay on the History of Civil Society*, Ferguson discusses the advantages wich we derive from society and he says: "We need not enlarge our communities, in order to enjoy these advantages. We frequently obtain them in the most remarkable degree, where nations remain independent, and are of small extent."[37] In the *Wealth of Nations* Smith argues that the Greek colonies succeeded because "they were at liberty to manage their own affairs in the way they judged was most suitable to their own interest," and that those of the Romans were much less successful because they did not have that liberty.[38]

Linda Colley in her book, *Britons: Forging the Nation: 1707-1837*, has argued that the idea of Britain was "an invention forged above all by war",[39] a Protestant struggle for survival against France as the foremost Catholic power. [There is an irony in this because the English brought about the

Union to prevent Scotland reviving the separate monarchy and perhaps the alliance with France.] Scottish Protestantism was very different from the English and France was Scotland's oldest ally. Even so, distrust of Catholicism was at least as strong in Scotland as in England and war against a common foe is a unifying force. You can see the growth of a British nationalism in, for instance, the Introduction to the first canto of Walter Scott's *Marmion*; but that did not stop him from making a passionate protest in the *Malachi* letters against English interference in Scottish affairs. Even Burns indulged in Britishness in "Does Haughty Gaul Invasion Threat?"— but probably only to calm the nerves of his superiors in the Excise.

The war against France was accompanied by the acquisition and consolidation of a great empire. Quebec was seized in 1759 and the battle of Plessey in 1757 led to Clive's conquest of Bengal. When George III came to the throne in 1760, George Macaulay Trevelyan has written, "Britain was held, perhaps, in higher esteem by the nations of the world than ever before or since. Her free institutions, imperfect as we know them to have been, were regarded with envy by the European nations of that day."[40] It is probably not a coincidence that it was precisely at this time that Boswell and Smith tell us that the Union had become acceptable.

The growth of the empire made a radical difference to Scotland's relationship with England and therefore to Scottish attitudes to the Union. Scotland had in practice limited autonomy, but no government of her own to promote development and legislate when necessary. There was, however, an educational system which produced more trained minds, administrators, doctors, teachers, soldiers and engineers than could be used at home. Great numbers of them found opportunities in the empire, which became a vast English-Scottish joint venture in which Scotland played a disproportionately large part. Within Scotland, industry was largely directed to an imperial market.

While the empire lasted, it became for the Scots an alternative source of pride, a substitute and compensation for the loss of independence. The empire, not the United Kingdom, became the substance and justification for the Union. As it happens, two distinguished historians have recently reached this same conclusion. Michael Lynch in *Scotland: A New History* writes of the rapturous embrace made by the Scots, not of Britain, but of a British Empire, which opened up in the 1780s and disappeared after 1945".[41] Linda Colley, in the book from which I have already quoted, says:

A British imperium... enabled Scots to feel themselves peers of the English in a way still denied them in an island kingdom. The language bears this out very clearly. The English and the foreign are still all too inclined to refer to the island of Great Britain as "England". But at no time have they ever customarily referred to an *English* empire.[42]

Clearly then we have now reached a new, and perhaps final, phase in the history of the Union and of Britishness. They have rested on four props. Two of them, the empire and war against France in defence of Protestantism, mercifully no longer exist. The other two, respect for the monarchy and for the British Parliamentary system, are now very precarious. Even the degree of *de facto* autonomy, which Scotland has enjoyed since the Union, has been largely demolished by the Thatcher and Major governments. Residual loyalties and old habits no doubt still remain, but the logic of the situation is that Scotland should return to its historic role in Europe.

At the beginning of this paper I mentioned the close links which bound Scotland to the rest of Europe before 1603. We were consummate Europeans, trusted so much that for centuries we provided the guards of the Kings of France and Scots were in the service of other countries as generals, admirals and ambassadors. The association was also intellectual. Scots could be found all over Europe as professors and students. Sixteen of them were Rectors of the University of Paris between its foundation and the Reformation. It was these circumstances which led to our belief in the virtues of a diversity of small independent nations, devoted not to expansion, but to co-operation.

It is in that conviction that many of us hope to see Scotland a full member of the European Union with the same degree of independence as any other member state. We believe that we have much to contribute as well as gain from the restoration of Scotland to the status of a normal European country.

References

1   P Hume Brown, *The Union of 1707* by various hands,
    introd.Brown (Glasgow 1907), p4.

2   William Robertson, *History of Scotland* (20th edition, London
    1817), iii p192

3   Murray Pittock,*The Invention of Scotland* (London 1991), p32.

4   Robert Wodrow, *Early Letters (1698-1709)*, ed. L W Sharp
    (Edinburgh 1937), p291.

5   Andrew Fletcher of Saltoun, (attributed), *State of the Controversy
    Betwixt United and Separate Parliaments* (1706) ed. Paul H. Scott
    (Edinburgh 1982), p24.

6   Bruce Lenman, *The Jacobite Rising in Britain 1689-1746*
    (London 1980), p87.

7   Earl of Mar and Kellie, *Manuscripts* (Historical Manuscripts
    Commission), (London 1904), p447.

8   David Daiches, *The Paradox of Scottish Culture* (Oxford 1964), p66.

9   *Ibid*. p27.

10 James Boswell, *Boswell in Holland* (London 1952), p161.

11 James Boswell, *The Applause of the Jury* (London 1981), pp60,
    264, 304.

12 James Boswell, *The English Experiment* (London 1986),
    pp10, 286.

13 James Boswell, *Boswell on the Grand Tour*, Germany (London
    1953), p218.

14 James Boswell, *Tour to the Hebrides* (Oxford 1934), p184.

15 James Boswell, *The Great Biographer* (New York 1989), p39.

16 James Boswell, *The Applause of the Jury* (London 1981), pp83-4.

17 James Boswell, *Laird of Auchinleck* (New York 1977), p66.

18 P Hume Brown, *The Legislative Union of England and Scotland*
    (Ford Lectures 1914) (Oxford 1914), pp4-5

19 William Wolfe, *A Look at the Scottish Psyche: an Interview by
    George* Byatt (Bathgate 1992), p2.

20 David Hume, *Selected Essays*, edd.Stephen Copley and
    Andrew Edgar (Oxford 1993), p175.

21   *Ibid*. p297.
22   David Hume, *Letters*, ed. J Y F Greig (Oxford 1932), i p436.
23   *Ibid*. ii p208.
24   *Ibid*.ii p209
25   *Ibid*.i p470
26   Nicholas Phillipson, *Hume* (London 1989), pp11-2.
27   James Boswell, *Boswell on the Grand Tour, Italy* (London 1955), p226.
28   Adam Smith, *The Wealth of Nations* (London 1971), i p68.
29   *Ibid*. i p216.
30   *Ibid*. ii. p204
31   *Ibid* ii p427.
32   Sir Walter Scott, *The Letters of Malachi Malagrowther*, ed Paul H Scott (Edinburgh 1981), p10.
33   Robert Fergusson, *Poems*, ed.Mathew McDiarmid (Edinburgh, Scottish Text Society, 1956), ii p143.
34   Robert Burns, *Letter to Mrs Dunlop*, National Library of Scotland, Accession 8810, (Text in A Scottish Postbag, edd. George Bruce, Paul H Scott: Edinburgh 1986).
35   David Hume, *Selected Essays*, edd. Stephen Copley, Andrew Edgar (Oxford 1993), p311.
36   *Ibid*. p64.
37   Adam Ferguson, *An Essay on the History of Civil Society*, 1767 (Edinburgh 1966), p39.
38   Adam Smith, *op.cit.*,ii pp64-5
39   Linda Colley, *Britons: Forging the Nation, 1707-1837* (Yale 1992), p5.
40   George Macaulay Trevelyan, *History of England* (London 1937), p545.
41   Michael Lynch, *Scotland: A New History* (London 1991), pxiv.
42   Linda Colley, *op.cit.*p130.

The Essential Scotland

Address to Royal Philosophical Society of Glasgow, March, 1996

When I decided to speak about the essential Scotland what I had in mind was an attempt to see if it was possible to identify characteristics which make Scotland, or rather the Scots, distinctive. We tend to assume that Scotland is a nation which is different from others. Can we demonstrate that it is and describe its particular qualities? Almost as soon as I decided to think about this, I came across a newspaper article by Robert Crawford, the poet and Professor of Modern Scottish Literature at St. Andrews. At first glance, he seemed to be asserting the futility of the whole exercise even before I had started:

> If we think in terms of one essential Scotland, unchanging through the ages, we are deluding ourselves and thrusting a death-mask on our culture. This is the fallacy of essentialism. Literature shows us metamorphic Scotlands, not a fossil nation...What we can learn from our literature is that Scotland changes, not that it stays the same.

Of course, Crawford is right about change. We all know from our own experience that in all aspects of life change is constant and irresistible and this certainly applies to national characteristics, or at least some of them. Hamilton Fyfe's book, *The Illusion of National Character*, published in 1940, was highly praised by such men as Bernard Shaw, H. G. Wells and C. E. M. Joad. The title itself was something of an illusion for Fyfe did not attempt to show that there was no such thing as national character. He assumed that it did exist as in such a passage as this: "In that century there were also seen the beginnings of the South American nations. Spaniards interbred with Indians. The resulting strains were neither Spanish nor Indian. All can perceive that the Argentines, Chileans, Bolivians, Uruguyans are different from both". His argument, like Crawford's, is essentially that national characters are subject to change. He also makes the points that there are always exceptions and that environment is a more important influence than heredity.

Except in that last particular, Fyfe's analysis is not dissimilar from one of the earliest discussions of the subject, David Hume's essay, "Of National Characters". Hume begins by saying that "the vulgar are apt to carry all national characters to extremes... they will admit of no exceptions". He continues: "Men of sense condemn these undistinguished judgements; though, at the same time, they allow that each nation has a peculiar set of manners, and that some particular qualities are more frequently to be met with among one people than among their neighbours." Later in the essay he remarks that "the manners of a people change very considerably from one age to another". I think that these are good working assumptions with which to approach the subject.

Hume distinguishes between the "moral" and the "physical" causes which affect these national characters. The "moral" he defines very widely as embracing the nature of the government, relations with neighbouring countries, plenty or penury and such like. "Physical" he describes as "qualities of air and climate". He denies that they have much influence, although towards the end of the essay he seems to assume the opposite, a point to which I shall return. Hume was writing some 40 years before Montesquieu in his *De l'Esprit des Lois* discussed the way in which these physical causes gave a people a distinct character and spirit.

Both Hume and Montesquieu seem to assume that despite the changes and the exceptions a sufficient core of identity remains to be recognisable over a substantial period. Is there perhaps an analogy with the evolution of the individual? Plato says in the *Symposium*: "Even in the life of the same individual there is succession and not absolute unity; a man is said to preserve his identity, and yet in the short interval which elapses between youth and age he is undergoing a perpetual process of loss and reparation". We all know that only too well. Still our friends and acquaintances are usually recognisable even after a lapse of years and it is rare for anyone to change radically in character. Is that true of countries as well? Are there characteristics of the Scots which have persisted over decades or even centuries?

In looking for an answer we should begin by considering the major factors which are likely to have had an influence. The first and most obvious of these is the geographical position and the climate that follows from it.

Scotland is a small, largely mountainous country, at the northern end of an island on the north-west fringe of Europe. It is exposed on one side to the Atlantic Ocean and on the other to the North Sea. It has a climate which is frequently ungenial in the winter and sometimes even in summer, but it is not extreme. A living can be wrested from the land and the sea, but it requires effort. At the end of his essay, although he had denied that the climate had much influence, Hume says that "people in very temperate climates are the most likely to attain all sorts of improvement". I suspect that he was thinking of Scotland. He had a high opinion of Scottish achievement, not unnaturally in the middle of the Scottish Enlightenment, — "the People most distinguish'd for literature in Europe", as he remarked in a letter to Gilbert Elliot.

Hume's explanation of the effect of a temperate climate on character is curiously limited to its influence on sexual mores, "their blood not being so inflamed as to render them jealous", as he says, "and yet being warm enough to make them set a due value on the charms and endowments of the fair sex." Other consequences are more far reaching. It is a climate which does not make human effort on the land and sea (for long the only sources of food and wealth) either hopeless or unnecessary. In Scotland, fruit does not fall from the trees without human labour and the conditions are arduous enough to encourage strenuous effort and co-operation between neighbours.

This Scotland was once a separate piece of land which in the course of geological time happened to come to rest against another piece of land now known as England. It had a separate identity even in those distant times; but it has also had a political identity, of a varying nature, as far back as history goes within virtually the same border. The Romans tried to add it to their Empire, but failed to hold it for any length of time. Hadrian's Wall, which they built to the south of it to mark the limit of their Empire, is parallel and close to the present Border which has therefore existed for about 2,000 years.

Within this border the people are of diverse origins: the tribes who resisted the Romans whom we call the Picts; the Gaelic-speaking Scots from Ireland who gave their name to the country; the Vikings who settled particularly in the islands to the north and west; the Germanic invaders who settled in the south-east of Scotland as well as all over England. The last of these brought the language which developed into both English and Scots. In Scotland the Scots language gradually began to displace Gaelic. At a much later stage, as a result of the association with England through the Reformation and the Unions of the Crowns and Parliaments, English became the dominant language in government, law and education. Gaelic and Scots have never ceased to be used both in literature and speech. To these should be added Latin. Although they had been outside the Empire, the Scots for centuries had a respect and affection for the Latin language which was long used in literature and even longer in education. The first translation of Vergil's Aeneid into any modern language was by Gavin Douglas in the 15th century into Scots. In the next century George Buchanan was widely regarded as the best Latin poet in post-classical times. His memorial window in Greyfriars Kirk in Edinburgh says that Scotland was the boundary of the Roman Empire, but the last refuge of Latin eloquence. Scotland therefore has always been a country of diverse population and several languages. For some centuries the Lowlands and the Highlands were divided from one another by different languages and different institutions and habits. This diversity of language and origin perhaps disposed the Scots to association and intercourse with other countries, and the early cultivation of Latin was a key to intellectual exchange with the rest of Europe.

There was another factor which encouraged the Scots to find friends and allies in the rest of Europe. Hume mentioned "the situation of the nation with regard to its neighbours" as one of the factors which created a national character. In the case of Scotland, there is no doubt that the pressure of our nearest neighbour has had many consequences, some perhaps beneficial, but others certainly catastrophic. The English kings and ruling classes in the Middle Ages were ruthless, acquisitive and aggressive. They repeatedly attacked and attempted to subdue, with varying degrees of success, every other country that was within their reach; Scotland, Wales, Ireland and France. In Scotland the attack began in 1296 with Edward I's sack of Berwick, then the largest and wealthiest town in Scotland. These attempts continued for the next 300 years. As late as 1545, the Earl of Hertford reported to Henry VIII that he had "brent, raced and cast downe" 7 monasteries (which included the great Border Abbeys), 16 castles, 5 market towns (which included Edinburgh, Leith and St. Andrews) and 243 villages.

In this long war, Scotland had two disadvantages. First of all, it was smaller, less populous and less wealthy than England. Secondly, the most prosperous and fertile part of Scotland, unlike England, lay immediately exposed to the invader with no natural obstacle across the east coast route to the capital. It was this part of Scotland that was repeatedly laid waste and Scotland suffered several disastrous defeats and heavy loss of life. Scotland was a flourishing Renaissance kingdom under James IV, but it never recovered from Flodden. John Grierson wrote: "We were driven into the wilderness of national poverty at Flodden by the English and the English never let us out of it to this day."

Added to the trials of the climate, therefore, the Scottish people had to contend with this repeated devastation and slaughter. They showed remarkable resilience in their response. The losses were incalculable, but paradoxically they were also benefits. It consolidated the people in a feeling of national community and solidarity, and a commitment to liberty, which cut across the class distinctions of the feudal system. The resistance to Edward I under Wallace was a popular resistance. The historian, George Macaulay Trevelyan, said of it:

> This unknown knight...had lit a fire which nothing since has ever put out. Here in Scotland, contemporaneously with very similar doings in Switzerland, a new ideal and tradition of wonderful potency was brought into the world; it had no name then, but now we should call it democratic patriotism. It was not the outcome of theory. The unconscious qualities of a people had given it reality in a sudden fit of rage. Theories of nationhood and theories of democracy would follow afterwards to justify or explain it. Meanwhile, it stood up, a fact.

The modern ideas of democracy (as distinct from those of classical Greece), of egalitarianism and nationalism owe much to the people of Scotland and Switzerland. They found their first and most eloquent expression in the Declaration of Arbroath of 1320, where national freedom is put before loyalty to the King, even when he was Robert the Bruce.

Scotland's need to find allies against such a powerful and aggressive neighbour led to a very close association with other countries in Europe. The alliance with France of 300 years is one of the longest in European history. It was so close that the countries exchanged citizenship and Scotland provided the guard of the French Kings. But it was not only with France. As merchants, pedlars, soldiers and scholars, Scots were at home in nearly every country of Europe. Before the Reformation, Scotland had a close relationship with the Vatican who regarded the Church of Scotland as a "special daughter". In many countries Scots were so valued and trusted that their governments appointed them as their ambassadors, admirals or generals, a very unusual tribute. Take as examples George Keith, 10th Earl Marischal, and his younger brother, James. Both had to leave Scotland because of their Jacobitism. George became Prussian Ambassador to France and then to Spain. He was also the Governor of Neufchatel and the only man that Rousseau seems to have admired and trusted. James was a general in the Russian service and then a Prussian field-marshal and one of their national heroes. In the universities of Europe Scots were prominent both as students and teachers. Between its foundation and the Reformation at least 17 Scots were Rectors of the University of Paris. Dugald Stewart believed that a cause of the "outburst of genius" in Scotland in the second half of the 18th century was the "continual intercourse from time immemorial between Scotland and the Continent" and "the constant influx of information and liberality from abroad". It is not surprising that Andrew Fletcher of Saltoun, the most robust defender of the independence of Scotland in the Scottish Parliament of 1703 to 1707, was also one of the first advocates of European co-operation. Scots have been good Europeans for centuries.

Another important, but fluctuating, element in the development of the national character is the influence of religion. Before the mid-16th century Scotland was, of course, Catholic, and this contributed to the association with the rest of Europe. The Reformation in Scotland was thoroughgoing, an example of the Scottish tendency to follow thought to its logical conclusion in preference to fudge or compromise. The reformed, Presbyterian Kirk was embraced with enthusiasm by many Scots for the next four centuries. Its structure reflected the same instinctive preference, which we have already noted, for egalitarian democracy. A central belief was the equality of all people before God. Hierarchy was rejected and replaced by a system of representative bodies, culminating in the General Assembly, which was more democratic than any Parliament at that time and for long afterwards. In the services of the Kirk there was a strong intellectual content with more emphasis on logical persuasion than on ritual, rhetoric or emotion.

Consistently with this, the Reformation gave an increased impulse to education. There were already universities in St. Andrews, Glasgow and Aberdeen and schools attached to the cathedrals and in many of the burghs. The First Book of Discipline of 1561, which laid down the ideals and aspirations of the Reformed Kirk, aimed at a school in every parish, one teaching Latin in every town, and a college in the ten larger burghs. From then onwards the Scottish Parliament repeatedly legislated towards the same end. Consequently, education was spread through the whole population in Scotland long before, even centuries before, other countries. There was a strong emphasis also on a rigorous, puritanical moral code and a distrust of ornament and ostentation. The ideal was plain living and high endeavour. At its height, music, dance, poetry and theatre were discouraged and in these there was a marked decline from the achievements of the mediaeval kingdom.

All of these ideals were a powerful influence in Scotland for at least 400 years. In the 17th century many Scots were prepared to risk persecution and death for the Covenants, which were a rejection of attempts by the King's government to interfere in religious matters. Even in the 19th century a similar spirit persisted. Let me give two examples. In 1798 a young English clergyman came to Edinburgh as a tutor to an English student at the University. He was Sydney Smith, who helped to found the *Edinburgh Review* and was afterwards well known as a wit and letter-writer. One of his early letters gives his first impressions of the Scots:

> In Scotland the Clergy are extremly active in the discharge of their functions, and from the hold they have on the minds of the people a very important body of men. The common people are extreemly conversant with the Scriptures, are really not so much pupils, as formidable critics to their preachers; many of them are well read in controversial divinity. They are perhaps in some points of view the most remarkable nation in the world, and no country can afford an example of so much order, morality, economy, and knowledge amongst the lower classes of society. Every nation has its peculiarities, the very improved state of the common people appears to me at present to be the phenomenon of this country.

My other example relates to that extraordinary and significant event, the Disruption of 1843, when the Church of Scotland split almost in half over the refusal of the government in London to abolish the right of landowners to appoint ministers which had been imposed by the British parliament shortly after the Union of 1707. This controversy, Lord Cockburn wrote, was "incomprehensible" to the English. They had no tradition of hostility to patronage and the independence of a Church "cannot arise in a Church (like the Church of England) which acknowledges the Crown as its head". 450 ministers of the Church of Scotland therefore walked out of the General Assembly, abandoning their manses and their incomes. This sacrifice of their professional station, emoluments and all worldly interests, purely from the dictates of conscience was, said Cockburn, "one of the rarest occurrences in moral history. I know no parallel to it... It is the most honourable fact for Scotland that its whole history supplies. The common sneers at the venality of our country, never just, are now absurd."

The Disruption meant a radical change in the position of the Church of Scotland. It had been a unifying force with its General Assembly partly replacing the Parliament which had been lost. It had provided social services and was now distracted from this at a time when industrialisation and the concentration of people in the cities had greatly increased the need for them. The new Free Church built new churches and halls all over Scotland, a remarkable achievement, but also in itself an enormous distraction of money and effort. About the turn of the century protestantism lost its virtual monopoly because of the arrival of large numbers of Catholics from Ireland, Italy and Poland, who added a further and valuable diversity to the population.

The greatest change of all is increasing secularisation. Religion is no longer a major factor in Scottish life; fewer and fewer people now go to church and normal life no longer ceases on Sundays. Still many of the attitudes which the Kirk inculcated remain. There is a story about a conversation in Edinburgh some decades ago when the Churches of Scotland and England had been engaged in negotiations about co-operation and the English had proposed the adoption of bishops in Scotland. One of the speakers expressed his outrage at such a monstrous proposal. His friend said, "I agree, but why does it upset you? I thought you were an atheist." "Yes I am," was the reply, "but I reserve the right to be a Presbyterian atheist." That, I think is what many of us are. We do not go to church or accept its faith, but we do share its egalitarianism, preference for logic over emotion, regard for education, dislike of ostentation and waste, concern for moral standards. Distrust of the arts is, fortunately, no longer common, but you do still find it here and there.

Another major factor in the evolution of the Scottish character, next in importance to the Wars of Independence and the Reformation, has been the Unions of the Crowns and of Parliaments with England. When by a dynastic accident James VI inherited also the English throne in 1603 and flitted to

London, Scotland lost royal patronage of the arts, her international identity and control over foreign, trade and defence policy. State appointments, including the ministers in the Scottish Government, were made in London under English influence. As Hume Brown said, "Scotland had become a shrivelled and a withered branch and her people knew it." The Scottish Parliament in 1703 and 1704 attempted to escape from this remote and damaging control, but it was in a weak position to resist the English insistence on an incorporating Union. England at last achieved her ambition to subordinate Scotland and remove any possible threat on her northern border.

This Union was highly unpopular in Scotland for about the next 50 years; but after the ruthless suppression of the '45 made it plain that escape was unlikely, people gradually accepted it. Over the course of the next 20 years or so Scots played an active part in the development and defence of the British Empire which the Union had made possible. Scottish attention turned away from Europe, even to an extent from Scotland itself, towards Canada, Africa, India, Burma, Hong Kong, Australia and New Zealand. Scottish industry, still mainly Scottish owned and managed, was directed towards trade with the Empire for which we built the ships and locomotives, and for which we supplied many of the politicians, administrators, traders, teachers, doctors andd soldiers.

This absorption in a British state, in which Scotland had no Parliament as a focus of its national life and identity, and no international identity either, might easily have led to the disappearance of the very idea of Scotland as a nation. As the *Claim of Right* of 1988 said, "The Union has always been, and remains, a threat to the survival of a distinctive culture in Scotland." The most obvious indication of the power of this threat is the displacement for most purposes of the Scots and Gaelic languages, which embody Scottish attitudes and associations, by the English of England. That a distinctive culture, and the national character associated with it, have in fact survived is a proof of its strength, but it has been sustained by several factors. In the first place, although the Unions of 1603 and 1707 deprived Scotland of political power, they left most Scottish institutions intact. They included the Church, the legal system, the burghs, the universities and schools. All of these, until quite recent times, had much more effect on the daily lives, habits and ideas of the people than the activities of a remote Parliament. Lindsay Paterson in his recent book, *The Autonomy of Modern Scotland* has argued that Scotland, at least before Thatcher, had as much *de facto* independence as many nominally independent countries.

Scotland has also been fortunate in its writers. Ramsay, Fergusson, Burns, Scott, Galt, Hogg, Stevenson, Garioch, Gunn, Linklater, Gibbon, Maclean, Gray, and scores of others, expressed and fortified the Scottish identity and reminded the world of our existence. If sometimes underground, the great body of Scottish folk-song, Scots and Gaelic, continued as a powerful assertion of it. The symbols of tartan and the bagpipes, although unreasonably distrusted by some people in Scotland itself, were recognised in the rest of the world as a sign of a distinctive tradition. Their adoption by the whole of Scotland is an indication also of the reconciliation of the Highlands and Lowlands.

We have, of course, paid a price for the Union. As Linklater concluded in his book on the subject, "people degenerate when they lose control of their own affairs" and that "by reason of its association with England, Scotland became insular. It substituted an English culture for that diversity of cultures with which in earlier times Scotland had always been in contact." In a book published in 1982 C J Watson suggested that you could find in Scotland "the sense of weariness, of the absence of hope, and of lacerating self-contempt which is a marked component in the psyche of 'colonised' people". You may think that this an exaggeration, but there is no doubt that there have been signs of a lack of self-confidence, and indeed of self-contempt, in contemporary Scotland. The Referendum of 1979 was an indication of it. In spite of the false promise from Lord Home which confused the issue, and the fact that there was a majority in favour, the outcome was hesitant. The opponents had succeeded in exploiting an underlying lack of confidence.

It is strange that Scotland should lack confidence in itself since our achievements have been so remarkable. The English historian, J A Froude, said, "No nation in Europe can look back with more just pride on their past than the Scots". Perhaps he was thinking primarily of the resilience and courage of the resistance to 300 years of attack, but even in that period Scotland produced great poets, philosophers and architects. Napier, Watt, Hutton, Black, Clerk Maxwell, and scores of others have made discoveries of fundamental importance in the history of science. Harold Thompson said of the age of the Scottish Enlightenment that "to discover comparable achievements by so small a nation in so short a time we should have to go back...to the age of Pericles". I think that he had forgotten Renaissance

Florence, but these are the only possible comparisons. The explanation for this paradoxical weakness of confidence lies largely in our education system. It has been possible to proceed through it, from primary school to a post-graduate degree, and emerge in almost complete ignorance of the history and literature of our own country and with the impression that everything of importance happened somewhere else. This is an impression which is heightened by the domination by London of our television and much of our radio and popular press. There is enormous pressure to make us look at the world through English eyes. Gordon Donaldson, who was Historiographer Royal of Scotland until his death in 1993, has said that even Scottish historians had largely "capitulated to the English point of view" and that "in English eyes anything that is not English is peculiar; worse than that it is backward, if not actually barbarous". All of this might be designed to create a massive inferiority complex and to destroy our distinctive national character.

A quite false vision of the Scottish past has been widely accepted which has its origin in anti-Scottish and Unionist propaganda. This included the notion that Scotland before the Union was a particularly poor, brutal and primitive place. In fact at all periods Scotland compared favourably in civilisation and humanity with other countries. Alexander Grant in his volume in *The New History of Scotland* on the period, 1306 to 1469, says that Scotland was peaceful internally by both English and European standards. Gordon Donaldson said of Scotland in the 16th century that it "was rather a kindly place, and certainly a safer country to live in than many others". I think that is true of Scotland at most periods, except during invasions from the south.

Of course, there has also been resistance to the distortion and misrepresentation of the Scottish past and of Scottish culture. George Davie in his great book, *The Democratic Intellect*, said that the life of Scotland since the Union had been marked by "alternation between catastrophe and renaissance, in which the distinctive national inheritance was more than once brought to the very brink of ruin only to be saved at the last minute by a sudden burst of reviving energy". In the last 100 years we have had several of these bursts, each building on the achievements of the one before. Our universities no longer neglect Scottish culture. It is now generally accepted that the Scots and Gaelic languages should be encouraged and not denigrated and suppressed. Scottish historical scholarship is now more firmly established than ever before. Our literature, theatre, music and painting are flourishing. There is, in fact, now a solid revival in our self-awareness and self-confidence.

In Boswell's *Life of Johnson* he tells us of a Mr. Edwards who said: "I have tried hard to be a philosopher; but, I don't know how, cheerfulness was always breaking in." There is an element of this in the Scottish character. Such qualities as courage, resilience, moral concern, respect for logic and for education, dislike of ostentation and display are worthy; but they could be, and often are, bleak and forbidding. There is another side to all of this, and it is this which strikes you first when you come back to Scotland after an absence. I mean a genuine and spontaneous friendliness and helpfulness, along with a solid integrity. These qualities appear frequently in literature, especially in diaries and memoirs. I take an example from the 18th century. Benjamin Franklin wrote in 1760 to Lord Kames about the time which he had spent in Edinburgh:

> On the whole, I must say, I think the time we spent there, was six weeks of the densest happiness I have met with in any part of my life; and the agreeable and instructive society we found in such plenty, has left so pleasing an impression on my memory, that did not strong connexions draw me elsewhere, I believe Scotland would be the country I should choose to spend the remainder of my days in.

Walter Scott had a penetrating and comprehensive understanding of Scotland. Two remarks which he made about the Scottish character in the *Heart of Midlothian* seem to me particularly apposite. "The eagerness with which Scottish people met, communicate and ... assist each other", was, he says, "due to patriotism ... combined with a conviction, which, if undeserved, would long since have been confuted by experience, that the habits and principles of the nation are a sort of guarantee for the character of the individual." He added at a later point in the novel: "Perhaps one ought to be actually a Scotchman to conceive how ardently, under all distinctions of rank and situation, they feel their mutual connection with each other as natives of the same country." As I have said, there was a time when Highlander and Lowlander were divided by mutual distrust. G M Trevelyan remarked that they have been "united in a common national pride ever since the days of Sir Walter Scott", because Scott helped to consolidate it. I suppose that one of the reasons for this strong feeling of community is that Scotland is small enough for the mind to grasp and to make us all seem like neighbours. It is cemented also by the concern for equality and social justice.

One of the most frequently quoted observations about the Scottish character is a passage in Gregory Smith's book, *Scottish Literature; Character and Influence*, which was published in 1919:

> Perhaps in the very combination of opposites — what either of the two sir Thomases, of Norwich and Cromarty, might have been willing to call "the Caledonian antisyzygy" — we have a reflection of the contrasts which the Scot shows at every turn, in his political and ecclesiastical history, in his polemical restlessness, in his adaptability, which is another way of saying that he has made allowance for new conditions, in his practical judgement, which is the admission that two sides of the matter have been considered.

Smith goes on to consider the tendency of Scottish literature to combine the factual and the fantastic, the prosaic and the romantic; but he thought that this "clear contrair spirit" applied to the whole of Scottish life. This appears in many forms and not only between people but with the same individual at different times and moods. The Scot who is normally logical, practical and sceptical can also be emotional, romantic or sentimental. In this matter of national character we are dealing with broad tendencies which are always subject to exceptions. We can expect to find no more than, in Hume's phrase, "that some particular qualities are more frequently to be met with among one people than among their neighbours".

I return now to the question with which we started. Are there some particular qualities among the Scots which have persisted in spite of inevitable change of circumstances? Considering, as I have been doing, Scottish attitudes and behaviour in different ages, it seems to me evident that there are tendencies which persist. Robert Crawford, in his essay which denied the whole idea, said that it is "an intellectual tangle" to call on Scottish literature to "demonstrate one constant and continuing tradition that is instinctively democratic". On the contrary, I think that this is one of the most obvious examples of a persistent theme. In Henryson's fable, *The Wolf and the Lamb*, in the 15th century, he tells us that the lamb represents the poor man and the wolf the overbearing rich, and there is no doubt where his sympathies lie. So in one of the earliest of Scottish poems we have the themes of social justice and the defence of the poor. The same thing is true of Lindsay's Johne the Common-weill in the *Thrie Estaites* in the 16th century, and of Burns's *For a' that and a' that* ("A man's a man for a' that") in the 18th, and of MacDiarmid, Garioch, Gray or almost all of our novelists and poets in the 20th. Walter Scott described himself as a Tory, but all of his most admirable characters, Edie Ochiltree or Jeanie Deans for example, are poor, simple people. Concern for social justice is evident, not only in our literature of all periods, but in the legislation of the Scottish Parliament before 1707, in the activities of the Churches, and in political movements which gathered pace from the early 19th century down to the refusal of the Scots to accept the ideology of Margaret Thatcher.

Henryson's lamb appeals to logic, the law and the scriptures and wins the argument, although that does not deter the wolf. You might say that already in the 15th century we have an early instance of the democratic intellect. The high esteem in which education is held in Scotland is seen in the early foundation of universities, the education act of James IV, the First Book of Discipline, the legislation of the Scottish Parliament, the tradition of the lad o pairts, and the demonstration against cuts in education by 40,000 people in Edinburgh in February this year (1996).

Michael Lynch ends the Introduction to his excellent *Scotland: A New History* (London 1991)with this sentence: "The pursuit of the intellect has long been a very Scottish obsession; it was also, for the Scots, a very European phenomenon." Our involvement in Europe before the Unions was a vital factor in our intellectual and artistic achievements because of our open-minded approach and readiness to react to the stimulus of new ideas from other countries. When we were diverted from Europe by the Unions with England, we showed a similar adaptability throughout the Empire. Now that the Empire no longer exists, I think that we are ready and eager for direct involvement again in Europe. To quote Michael Lynch once more, the Scottish National Party's policy of independence in Europe "re-establishes one of the most important threads of continuity in Scottish history".

I think that George Davie was right when he said that Scotland is a nation which has made a "distinctive and fundamental contribution" to civilisation and this derives from that combination of egalitarianism, respect for intelligence and education and receptiveness to new ideas, which he has called the democratic intellect. This is one of the very strong reasons why I should like to see Scotland recovering her independence. It would allow these distinctive and valuable qualities to develop untrammeled and undistorted for our own benefit and the benefit of other countries as well.

The Cringe is the Enemy

Paper for the Advisory Council for the Arts in Scotland and Saltire Society Conference on "Arts, Democracy and the Scottish Parliament", Edinburgh University, 24th January, 1998.

There was a discussion recently on Radio Scotland about the reasons for the poor international performances of our football and rugby teams. Everyone seemed to agree that the basic reason was low expectation because of low self-esteem. Scottish teams did not win because they expected to lose. If this applied only to sport, it might be a pity, but it would not be a disaster. The trouble is that demoralising self-depreciation is evident in many aspects of Scottish life. Wide-spread ignorance about our past achievements and present strengths is both a cause and a result of this malaise. Many Scots seem to assume that everything in Scotland from literature, painting and music to cooking and the climate is inferior to the equivalents in other countries. It is the attitude which has been called the Scottish Cringe. This is a phrase which I dislike and do not normally use; but I have to admit that there are people for whom it is the only appropriate description. One of the signs of the condition is a tendency to give senior posts, even in functions closely involved with our national identity, to people bred in a different tradition.

Scotland looks like a text-book demonstration of the theory which Frantz Fanon advanced in relation to France and her former colonies, Michael Hechter in what he called the "internal colonialism" of the British Isles and Craig Beveridge and Ronald Turnbull in the particular case of Scotland itself. This the theory of "inferiorisation", the idea that imperial expansion involves the disparagement of the cultures of dominated peoples in order to justify the domination and weaken the will to resist. It is a process which is largely carried out through the voluntary co-operation of a privileged élite within the dominated territory.

We are all familiar with the activities of such an élite in Scotland, always ready to disparage anything Scottish as parochial but to fawn on the superior wisdom and taste of parochial London. I do not think that there is the slightest evidence to suggest a deliberate English plot to disparage Scottish culture. That was not necessary, given the supreme confidence of their own élite and the ready admiration and imitation of it by some influential people in Scotland. The real question is why did this happen in a country which in the past had a good conceit of itself and which has an impressive record of achievement in the arts, philosophy, sciences and almost every other human activity? We have to go back three of four centuries to find an answer.

The process began in 1603 when royal patronage was removed to London in the baggage of James VI. Men of ambition with their eyes on court favour had to ape the language and manners of the dominant class in London. The removal also of the Parliament to London through the Union of 1707 applied this pressure to everyone with political ambition. Hope of escape from the Union vanished with the defeat of the Rising of 1745 and the ruthlessness of its suppression. By about 1760 many people in Scotland had come to the conclusion that the only practical policy was *if you can't beat them, join them.* They set about following this policy to its logical conclusion, which is the Scottish habit.

One aspect of this was their attitude to language and that is crucial. All languages embody centuries of shared experience and for this reason each of them is the only adequate means of expressing the attitudes which derive from that experience. D D Devlin makes the point in his book, *The Author of Waverley*: "It is often remarked that Scott's strength lies in the handling of the vernacular. What perhaps needs saying is that his strength lies here not simply because he had an ear for Lowland speech, but because he endorsed these qualities of mind and character which the vernacular so accurately conveyed." Or, as Iain Crichton Smith said recently in a television programme, "If you lose your language, you lose your world." He was in this case referring to Gaelic, to which the same considerations apply. Our schools for centuries have done their best to destroy both Scots and Gaelic. Perhaps this was done with good intentions (your voluntary co-operation again), but these teachers were destructive in more ways than one. They were undermining the culture and the self-confidence of their pupils and often their ability to express themselves in any language at all. They were saying in effect the language which you bring from your parents is inferior and unacceptable and so therefore is the whole culture which it expresses.

This policy of the schools derives from an idea which gripped the literati of the Scottish Enlightenment from about 1760. They persuaded themselves that Scots was, in David Hume's words, "a very corrupt dialect" and that they had to go to great efforts to acquire the written and spoken language of polite circles in London. Hume's remark reveals an ignorance of linguistic history, but apart from that I think that many complicated motives were at work. The idea that there should be one classical and correct standard of most things was a prevalent notion at the time. The literati wanted their books to be acceptable to the English, as well as the Scottish, market. From the time of James VI, English prose had acquired prestige in Scotland through the translation of the Bible which he had authorised; but Scots had a much stronger tradition in verse than in prose. Still, the deliberate effort, requiring great pains, to unlearn your own native speech and acquire that of a neighbouring, and traditionally hostile, country is a strange penomenon which needs a fuller explanation.

It is true that, there was also, as Charles Jones says in the *Edinburgh History of the Scots Language*, a nationalist backlash: "There was a strong sense in Scottish intellectual circles that Lowland Scots had a long and respectable pedigree and that it had produced an outstanding literary tradition." The poets, Allan Ramsay, Robert Fergusson and Robert Burns, wrote in Scots and were outspoken in their detestation of the Union. Then and since there tends to be an affinity between the literary use of Scots and cultural and political nationalism.

The decision of the literati to accept the fact that the Union was then inescapable did not affect only their language. You might well get the impression from many of their books that they had embraced the British state so wholeheartedly that they wanted to forget Scotland all together. They seem deliberately to avoid all reference to Scotland, even when that would be appropriate, by drawing their historical examples from England, ancient Greece and Rome or North America. Their letters which were not intended for publication give a very different impression. Hume's for instance, are full of a robust Scottishness and his references to the people whom he called "the Barbarians who inhabit the banks of the Thames" are anything but complimentary.

There are discreet, but clear, hints here and there in the books of the literati that they agreed with Andrew Fletcher that countries should remain small and independent. In other words, they too regretted the Union. Hume in one of his *Essays* says that "a small commonwealth is the happiest government in the world" and that "Freedom naturally begets public spirit, especially in small states". Adam Ferguson in his *Essay on the History of a Civil Society* says that communities need not be enlarged to enjoy the advantages of society: "We frequently obtain them in the most remarkable degree, when nations remain independent, and are of small extent." John Millar in his book, *The Origins of the Distinction of Ranks* says that the people of small states "have been commonly successful in their efforts to establish a free constitution", but that extensive nations were much more likely to end in tyranny.

It seems to me that these men disliked the Union, but felt that they should not make too much fuss about it. The way in which the Union had been achieved had been a traumatic experience for Scotland, but the aftermath of the '45 was still worse. If you now opposed the Union, you were liable to be accused of Jacobitism and treason. It was prudent to avoid the subject and sensible to try to make the best of it, in other words to accept Hanoverianism and Britishness and try to be as English as possible. Even Robert Burns, when he was threatened with a Government enquiry into his politics, decided to write a couple of letters and a poem or two saying the opposite to what he had believed all his life.

In spite of the originality and intellectual brilliance of the Enlightenment literati, therefore, there was a distinct element of cringe about their attitude to Scotland. Unfortunately it is this element, adopted for temporary but compelling historical reasons, which has affected Scottish education ever since. It has been focused on England rather than Scotland and has tended to give the impression that Scotland is an irrelevant backwater and that everything of importance has happened somewhere else. You might almost conclude that it had been designed to create an inferiority complex and destroy Scottish culture.

When broadcasting was introduced in the 1920s it might have become a powerful medium for Scottish self-expression. It was, however, a time when our confidence was at a low ebb and we allowed London to assume control. That is where it has remained, for radio and later, and to a greater extent, for television. This has strongly reinforced the impressions already created by our schools. I do not think that Geoffrey Barrow exaggerated when he said that our failure to create an autonomous broadcasting system was the most damaging blow to Scottish culture in a hundred years.

With such powerful forces opposed to our cultural identity, it is proof of its inherent strength that it has survived at all. Two factors have helped to sustain it. Our wealth of traditional music, song and dance has flourished more or less underground, in spite of official discouragement. More on the surface, but largely disregarded by the schools until quite recently, we have had a virtually continuous succession of writers whose work has kept the Scottish identity alive: Scott, Galt, Hogg, Stevenson, MacDiarmid, Smith, Garioch, MacLean, Mitchison, to name only a few, followed by the vibrant activity of the contemporary literary scene.

The report, *A Claim of Right for Scotland*, of July 1988, led to the Constitutional Convention and to the current Scotland Bill. It says (and who could deny it?) "The Union has always been, and remains, a threat to the survival of a distinctive culture in Scotland." The restoration of the Scottish Parliament should give us an opportunity to remove the adverse pressures on our cultural identity and on our self-confidence which is intimately connected with it. Admittedly the Bill proposes only a small first step. Such has been the frenzy of Whitehall Departments to retain their empires that the list of powers reserved to Westminster amounts to 18 pages. Outrageously and indefensibly, even broadcasting is reserved. Still even a limited Parliament is a step in the right direction and there is every opportunity for us all to press for the measures which we think are necessary.

This is a fundamental point. Without reasonable, but not excessive, self-esteem, neither an individual nor a country is likely to be able to achieve very much, culturally, economically, or in any other way. When Sir John Sinclair published the first *Statistical Account of Scotland* in 1791 he said that his object was to increase "the quantum of happiness enjoyed by its inhabitants". I think that should still be our overriding purpose and that the recovery of self-confidence is a necessary part of it. We shall have to work towards that, both through Parliament and through every other means available to us. I suggest six immediate objectives:

1   In spite of the Bill, perhaps the most urgent of all is real autonomy for BBC Scotland and the creation of a Scottish Broadcasting Authority.

2   The schools should be encouraged to give adequate attention to Scottish history, especially cultural history, languages, literature, ideas and social and economic conditions. Their aim should be to things and to make their pupils feel at home in Scotland.

3   The recommendations of the Universal Declaration of Linguistic
    Rights should be applied to Gaelic and Scots.
4   A Scottish National Theatre should be funded, along with the other
    national companies, directlyby a Ministry for the Arts.
5   We should follow the example of the Irish Republic in the
    encouragement of our traditional music and dance as a great national
    asset. A school for them should be established, preferably in a restored
    Linlithgow Palace.
6   An agency to foster cultural exchange between Scotland and other
    countries should be established.

Our main enemy is the Scottish Cringe. We should banish it for ever.

Some Other Saltire Publications

About the Saltire Society

The Saltire Society was founded in 1936 at a time when many of the distinctive features of Scotland's culture seemed in jeopardy. Over the years its members, who have included many of Scotland's most distinguished scholars and creative artists, have fought to preserve and present our cultural heritage so that Scotland might once again be a creative force in European civilisation. As well as publishing books the Society makes a number of national awards for excellence in fields as diverse as housing design, historical publication and scientific research. The Society has no political affiliation and welcomes as members all who share its aims. Further information from The Administrator, The Saltire Society, 9 Fountain Close, 22 High Street, Edinburgh. EH1 1TF Telephone 0131 556 1836.